Reflections

. . . a true story

Yashi

authorHOUSE®

AuthorHouse™
1663 Liberty Drive
Bloomington, IN 47403
www.authorhouse.com
Phone: 1-800-839-8640

Published by AuthorHouse   06/06/2012

ISBN: 978-1-4670-4425-7 (sc)
ISBN: 978-1-4670-4427-1 (hc)
ISBN: 978-1-4670-4424-0 (e)

Library of Congress Control Number: 2012909444

"Reflections" is dedicated to the inner warrior that
lies within each one of us.

Contents

Preface

*T*his book is an effort on my part to document my life's journey which like many of us, had its share of ups and downs. "Reflections" has helped me in achieving personal closure for a lot of tragedies I have been through. I have made every effort to present it as a motivational read. Writing this book was not easy. Since this is a memoir, it was emotionally very taxing at times to relive the past. I consider getting this book published, my biggest personal achievement so far.

I would take this golden opportunity to thank each and every person who has been a part of my life in any way, positive or negative. I am who I am because of my past.

First and foremost, this venture would not have been possible without the support of my family. Dad, thanks for teaching me the importance of discipline. Mom, I owe my writing skills to your genes. My sister Ritu, you are an inspiration and an epitome of resilience. My brother Manish, you are my mentor and guiding light in my tough times. My brother-in-law, Braj, you rock with your posh British ways and we will certainly celebrate this book's launch with your favorite champagne. My sister-in-law Roopam, you are the center of our family's universe. Thanks for being so kind and generous and most importantly, being you. I cannot dare to forget my maternal uncle with an evolved literary mind, uncle Jatinder.

Yashi

I would like to thank my pillars of strength, my nieces and nephews Raghav, Radhika, Ambika, Uday, Ansh, Annie, Vaishnavi, Seerat, Atharva, Gabriel, Anika, Ishika, Shaurya, Sahil, Sanjali, Golu, Siddharth, Uday Jr. and Asmi. You lovely flowers are my biggest stress busters and I cherish you.

This book's completion would not have been possible without the support of my Infosys co-workers and friends. I owe it to you all. Amy, Thanks for being the divine support for me, my friend. Garima, Guncha, Simer, Shruti Varma, Raaavi, Ridhima, Swati, Kriti, Nidhi Kapoor, Harry, Gagan, Alka, Pranjli, Gurleen, Pranky, Rabri, Sonia, Nitin and everyone on my FB friend's list. I love you all.

Charu Vohra, it is because of you my friend, I am "breathing" now. If not for my stay with you at New York, this book's publishing happened. Anuj Puri, thanks for not ever judging me. Chaya Mam, Harsimrat and Channi didi for lighting my life up. Thanks Dilli Mama for the yummy cheese dish every Monday. Komal Dani, Maddy, Paro, Smita and Kanika Sharma for being the best critics and an author's delight. Smriti Sharma for awakening the nation through the might of journalism.

I thank Rajat Gupta, Simer, Mukesh and Ajish for clicking my pictures used in this novel. The copyright of the images lie with the respective photographers. Some of the names, dates and events have been changed in order to protect the privacy of the parties involved and to align to the story in a better way.

I won't be justified if I don't thank my cousins who were always there, right by my side standing like a rock. HRH Minnie Di, for scolding me and encouraging me on a need basis. Homi, Shikha, Mukesh, Pooja, Chinu, Ghoga, Bitta, Ely; you all hold a special place in my heart.

My Slalom colleagues, you guys are the BEST in the world. I am very fortunate to know you all and to be able to address you as my friends. George, Bob, Brad, Brian and Jerry; Thanks for creating such a positive work environment for all of us and making Slalom Consulting "The Best Place to Work". You are the best bosses anyone can dream of.

Alli, Jen Owens, Catherine Golden, Becky Watson, DanO, Karunya, Annie Ezell; I am very lucky to have you all in my life. You make this world a better place. TiffanyN-I thank you for being a positive influence. You were extremely supportive in making me comfortable in this country and in Seattle. All of you are my oxygen.

All my teachers who have made me technically, morally and academically competent. Ms. Tajinder, Ms. Litt, Mr. Patial, Mr. Chawla, Ms. Nandita, Mr. Vinod, Mr. Ranjodh, Dr. Narinder Sandhu and Mrs. Saini for recognizing my potential and tapping my talents, a heartfelt gratitude.

Last but not the least; I want to thank Vijay and my Goddess Durga for bringing him and me together. You re-ignited my lost belief in love. You make me feel wanted and cared for. I love you and thanks for accepting me with all my flaws. I appreciate you as my best half.

Thank you all for your endless support and patience. You all make my life worth living.

REFLECTIONS

Part 1

*W*hen I think about my life's story, I often wonder when I should begin and when I should end.

I thought I was great company for others and used to steal the show whenever I wanted. Things were never difficult for me. Talking to strangers never made me nervous, and I made friends very easily. Life was nothing but fun.

My mimicry skills and clownish attitude won me many friends. I was a popular girl in my high school, because I was given numerous awards and honors for my participation in extracurricular activities. I also scored good marks in almost all subjects (except math).

Love for me was a very "filmy" thing. I thought the concept of love only suited Bollywood movies and nothing like "true love" existed in the real world. According to me, people who had premarital romantic affiliations were *bad* students and very *bad* sons and daughters. I thought they betrayed their parents every now and then for their own selfish, personal reasons, which were very difficult for me to comprehend at that particular time. I was merely in ninth grade, and that's what love meant for me.

It was when those green eyes entered my life in a very remarkable and dramatic manner, my attitude about love changed. It was the first ever school trip we had. It was enough to excite me that we would be visiting Rajasthan in India, "the land of the kings." We packed our bags and rushed to the railway station. I was so very unlike my friends, who were more excited about guys going along with us than visiting Rajasthan.

It was at the beautiful hill station called *Mount Abu* where I felt a shiver throughout my body and realized that something unusual was happening to me. I saw those beautiful, mysterious green eyes staring at me through a layer of amazing strands of hair running over the forehead and conveniently ending just on the level of those green eyes. That added even more mystery to the gazing pair. I was fantastically thrilled but shooed away the feeling as a negative one and tried to concentrate on the monuments and their history. I was even taking notes on what our guide was describing about the splendid *Dilwara Jain Temples*.

Whenever I noticed those intriguing green eyes, they pierced a part of me. The real *shock* as well as *surprise* (till then) of my life was yet to arrive. The next evening, we were scheduled to visit Sunset Point in Mount Abu. I felt the intense romance in the ambience captivating me. I was surprisingly searching for those green eyes. The thought of it was making me uncomfortable. I was so unsure about myself for the first time in my life.

Then, I noticed, by *choice*, of course, that amazing pair gazing at me so vividly. It seemed to me as an X-ray machine, though it wasn't intended to be that way. I found myself mesmerized by the sight of the sun setting so beautifully down the hills, playing hide and seek with the clouds and gradually disappearing. And I was even more spellbound with him staring at me with such amazingly high levels of interest. All through our exchange of stares I forgot to hang around by my other classmates and my teachers, and I even lost track of time. He was looking at me endlessly and finally smiled. It was then that I noticed a handsome strand of hair falling over on the right half of his forehead again and again and being blown away by the breeze repeatedly. Oh! I so much hated the breeze by then, I swear. The reason behind that hatred was not clear to me though.

Part 2

*B*oth of us were left alone (I said alone, as I wasn't even aware of his name till that moment). I saw him advancing towards me with a very cute smile, and it was becoming wider and wider as the distance between us was becoming less. It was giving me the best goose bumps I ever had. He came up to me and with a crisp sense of confidence introduced himself to me as he pushed out his right hand toward me with an obvious intent of a handshake.

My right hand just didn't listen to me and poured out against all my coy wishes and shook. Yes! It shook me from within. I noticed that his face had other features as well, like those beautiful luscious lips, that very much proportionate nose, not to mention that perfect pair of green eyes, which definitely, precisely gave my feelings the name of love. I was very sure then that it was nothing but love.

"Rahul," he said. "Hi! I am Rahul. Can we be friends?"

My orthodox Indian heart thumped even harder than 282 beats per minute. Each beat wanted to say, "Yes!" but somehow my lips didn't support me, and I answered in the form of a question. "Why?" I asked.

He tried to explain his point of view as to why friendship was an integral part of life. He said, "You are one of the most popular and charming girls of the school. You are a class apart when it comes to debates, poetry recitations, and dramatics."

Oh, man! I was so happy. I realized I had grown up to accept complements from guys, blush severely at the same time, and feel glad deep down inside.

A smile flashed on my seemingly frowning face. Rahul reciprocated with a smile. We again shook hands and realized that *we were lost*. It was very dark by that time, and I was as scared as hell. I prayed with all my soul, as it was anything but my idea of a perfect vacation to be lost somewhere in the hills of Mount Abu. I was in the midst of a thought hurricane when I heard a very shrilly voice screaming my name. I turned back and saw my teachers. Their faces were flaunting a strange expression of relief and anger.

Mrs. Khajuria asked, "Yashi! What are you doing here? Where were you? And you . . . What's your name? . . . Rahul. What are both of you doing here exactly? Please explain."

I became extremely nervous and answered, "Ma'am, I lost direction, and Rahul noticed me going the wrong way. So he followed me to bring me back. We were on our way back already. I am sorry for the inconvenience, ma'am." The statement I made was enough to bring a pat on Rahul's back. He became so elated after that, earning a friend and a pat within a matter of twenty minutes.

We climbed the bus steps only to encounter the interrogative eyes of all our friends. They were so inquisitive about why we were late.

My best friend Alka would just not leave me alone that day, if I didn't reenact every moment of that beautiful first meeting.

Our remaining trip passed on with all the glitz and glamour of the first love. Those ten days and ten nights transformed me completely. I felt like a woman, so complete in *most* of the respects.

Part 3

*M*y routine involving schools and studies resumed. Memories would never fade away. The first chirps of the love birds were heard by all my friends. Everything was the same except my heart, which transitioned from its orthodox form to a novel, in love, delicate one. I started believing that not all lies are bad and wrong. I used to visit Rahul's home during my after school private coaching timings. It was so much fun and a thrill skipping classes to be with him. Once I went to his home to study. He wanted me to give a nickname to him, and he would do the same for me. The condition attached was that it would not be shared with even our best friends. I told him to initiate this naming ceremony. (I found it a little stupid.) He told me since he thought my lips were the best in the world, he would name me Lips. I felt awkward at first, but it was gradually sinking in that maybe guys were like that.

Then it was my turn. Spontaneously, I replied, "Mahtaab."

He asked, "Mahtaab?! What does that mean?"

I answered, "Mahtaab means moon, Stupid."

He said, "Mahtaab is a beautiful name but why did you relate it to me darling?" To this day, I don't know why at all I named him that.

Life moved on, and our semester grades were out. My grades went down as the hormones grew. I was certainly maturing. With Rahul around, the natural process of the biological growth saw another perspective. It was somewhere around the winter of that year I totally grew up. I realized how different I was from Rahul. I was so disgraced for going through the pain of reaching puberty, which was only the beginning for any woman. At the same time, I was so jealous of Rahul.

"Why me?" was the question I asked over and over again. After a day of leave from school and certain Hindu rituals, my mom told me that now I had to be even more cautious from boys. She didn't tell me the exact reason, and I didn't ask. It was enough embarrassment for me for one day already.

The phone rang at about six thirty that night. It was my friend Alka. She wanted to know why I hadn't been at school that day. She had the right to inquire, as she was my best friend. She also did not hesitate to convey Rahul's message for me stating, "He missed you a lot today."

"I missed him as well," I told her.

Alka was a very positive, intelligent, and eloquent female. We competed against each other in school debates and loved to lose from each other. We shared almost all our secrets, and silly girl talks were a part of our daily hour-long conversations. I still remember all the anger of the world clubbed up in my dad's wrinkled and experienced face whenever he saw me on the phone. To him, teeny talks were a sheer *waste* (both in terms of money and time).

Today, I understand what hard-earned money means and how painful it is for the parents to watch their kids waste it. Rahul's dad also shared my dad's views, but his mom was a lot more liberal than my mom. One fine evening, his mom caught us talking on the phone. She picked up the extension connecting the same telephone line. There he was, as usual, praising my lips and telling me how desperately he wanted to feel them. I was reluctant about it then like most of the shy girls would be. It had been almost a year since we began dating. (Our first anniversary was approaching, and we were making big plans for that.)

Bang! I heard a door open at the other end of the phone line, and Rahul probably hid the receiver under his quilt but I was able to understand the conversation of my man with his mom.

"Who was that, Beta*?" his mom demanded to know.

"Who, Mom?! What are you talking about?"

"'Your luscious lips.' Who is it?" she asked again.

"Oh, man! How . . . how d-d-do y-you know this?" Rahul stuttered.

"I heard your conversation, Darling, and I completely understand that you are lonely in your life as I could not give you a brother or a sister. I wish that you would begin treating me as a friend from now on, as I didn't even realize that you have grown up to admire girls and even have a girlfriend."

Then there was a long pause.

"Excuse me, Mom! Please don't call her my girlfriend. It is and indecent word for the lovely relationship we share. *She is my life*," Rahul said.

I had tears of happiness touching my eyelids by that time. I felt the love taking away all the fears in him.

_____

* Beta: means 'Son' in Hindi language.

"Rahul! What is her name?" his mother asked.

"Yashi! Yashi is the name, Mom," he answered.

"I wish to meet her real soon, Beta."

I heard a million church bells ringing in my head.

Part 4

Rahul disconnected the phone and called me later that night. He asked me if I could talk. Since my big brother was around, I told him that I would see him the next day, and I hung up. I remember staring at the walls the entire night and not being able to sleep at all. For the first time in my life, I was unsure of how I would react when I saw him. After the morning assembly, we went on to attend our first class on the English language. I couldn't concentrate on the stupid story of some guy called Babuli and his brothers. Mrs. Surinder could see my lack of mental presence in the class and objected to the same. I somehow did not bother and was continuously gazing at the clock for the bell to ring so that we could all proceed for the PE period where we could be tortured by our sports teacher, Mr. KK, whom our seniors called Kukkad* for reasons unknown to us.

I said tortured, because he made us run in the hottest of the days for half an hour nonstop. If we halted, he yelled at us like an army commanders would at his troops. Many girls fainted in the process every week, but it didn't bother him at all. After that sweaty run, we were given half an hour to gossip and chitchat. That was the part I was actually looking forward to that day. I had to speak to Rahul about the last night's conversation.

_____
* Kukkad: means 'rooster' in Punjabi language

His mom wanted to see me ASAP. She and his dad were unaware that I had visited their home in their absence. Rahul's dad, being a doctor, was out of the house most of the time. His mom was very much involved in her social life. Kitty parties and card clubs were eminent parts of her routine. Her Kitty parties meant a private evening date for both of us in his home. Kitty parties are a very popular way that Indian housewives socialize. The ladies pool in some money and play poker. He asked me to meet his mom the following day. I was nervous and scared. Being in love teaches you how to have a perfect blend of emotions most of the time. Butterflies in my stomach gradually increased their size to that of the eagles. I asked Rahul what I should be wear for the occasion, which was going to change my life forever.

He suggested that I wear a salwar kameez** for the subsequent evening, but I protested. I was a tomboy famous for never wearing a traditional outfit—not that I had something against it, but I was not very comfortable carrying it. Moreover, at that time, I did not possess any Indian suits. Finally, it was decided that I would be wearing a decent top and a pair of denims. I clearly remember that skin-tight, stretchable jeans were popular in those days, and Rahul made me wear funny looking, baggy jeans, because he didn't want any tight pants on me for the big day.

The next evening finally arrived. I cycled on my magenta-colored Miss India bicycle to his house. The basket in front of the bike carried a bouquet for his mom that I had handcrafted myself.

I was very scared, because I thought I would not know what to say if she scolded us for not focusing on our studies. Some cells in my

---

** salwar-kameez: a traditional Indian outfit which is considered conservative and formal body were elated, because I realized that from that day onward, our relationship might turn formal. I rang the doorbell and set my blunt cut hair right for about what seemed like the millionth time.

There he was, looking at me from the corner of his eyes and opened the main door for me. He was one chivalrous guy who would hold it open until I enteredthe drawing room. He told me to be comfortable and made me sit on the sofa. I realized I was almost shivering in nervousness. Then his mom entered carrying a tray full of snacks and Pepsi. I stood up, and my hands automatically folded as a mark of respect.

"*Namaste! Beta, ji.* How are you doing?" she said to me.

I noticed a hint of stammer in my voice when I answered her. "I am very fine, Aunty*. How are you?"

She said, "I am fine, Darling! Please help yourself with the snacks."

The phone rang, and Aunty excused herself to receive it. Rahul judged that I was not very comfortable and followed his mom. Both of them emerged from the master bedroom in ten minutes. Aunty smiled at me and sat next to me. She ordered Rahul to go to the kitchen and get a glass of water for her. He went away. Aunty asked me about my hobbies and my family members. I told her that my dad was a retired army officer, and my mom was a homemaker. I mentioned that my elder brother was an engineer and that my sister, the eldest amongst us all, had received a double masters in human biology and human molecular genetics and was married to a solicitor in UK.

_____

* Aunty: In Indian culture, it is considered offensive to address elders by their name, hence we address them as 'uncle' and 'aunty'

Aunty was really impressed by the social and academic details of the family, I guess, as she said, "That means you must be a great student yourself as well!!"

I very much wanted to answer, "I was a great student once, but after meeting your son, I just cannot focus on my studies anymore." But I didn't.

The conversation evolved, and Aunty made me feel great about me and Rahul being together. She admitted that she initially thought that Rahul's love would be split up for her as I was there, but after meeting me, she was as elated as Rahul about me being in his life—or me *being* his life, as he portrayed.

I asked Aunty for her leave as it was getting dark and I wanted to hit the road at the earliest.

She said, "Beta, ji! I have a request. Please do not call me Aunty from now on. Please call me Mama, as it was my dream to have a lovely daughter like you, and please visit me soon again. It was so amazing for me to know you, Beta."

I was joyous at hearing what she said and promised her that I would call her Mama. We waved good-bye, and I noticed Rahul winking at me secretly and smiling at the same time as they came to see me off.

I went to my bed without finishing my homework. I was too busy thinking about my first meeting with my would-be mom-in-law who was so affectionate and gave my man his pair of green eyes. Rahul had the eyes of his mom (I loved Rahul's pair much more). Her fair and glowing skin and that motherly smile made me wonder if I had seen her before in some TV commercial. I slept over those thoughts and had a very well-deserved, sound sleep after two insomniac nights.

Part 5

$\mathcal{T}$ime flew by, and we (Rahul and I) didn't realize that the grade 10 board exams were over, and the fight began on what subjects to opt for college (eleventh and twelfth grade). I was skeptical to opt for the sciences, but my folks just didn't listen to me at all. To add to the misery, I had an elder sister (thirteen years older than me) and a brother (ten years older) who were my pseudo parents. I always felt that I was the unluckiest one when it came time for me to get permission for even the minutest of the things. Normally, kids seek permission from a single set of parents, whereas I had to get approval from three sets of parents (mom and dad; sister and Jiju [sister's hubby]; and brother and his fiancée). It was such a pain.

To add to my pains, my brother and I shared a lot in common. I discovered that he caught most of my lies without any special efforts. Monu (my elder brother) was always at a vantage point when it came to his dealing with me. When my sister Ritu got married (I was in grade VI then) and moved abroad, he became very protective of me. He was very strict with me for most of the things, like the time when I should be home, my hours of studying, the kind of magazines I read (I was never allowed to read *Teens Today*, as Monu thought it to be an inappropriate read for me (as it discussed sexual issues that teens faced), and, above all, what I watched on TV. Of course, my parents always supported him in whatever he said or did, as he was himself a great student and a very successful engineer and businessman.

Those days, a television show called *Hip Hip Hurray* got started It was a privilege to have a cable connection at home then. As I belonged to a family with elder siblings, we had a cable connection with a lot of restrictions on it for me. But I somehow managed to finish my homework early every Wednesday and sit in front of TV for *HHH*, as it was very popular among all the teenagers—especially the length of the skirts girls wore, which could never happen in reality in Indian schools. Once Monu sat with me watching *HHH*, and as soon as the episode finished, he announced that I was not supposed to watch it ever again, because it was inappropriate. I remember that I cried to sleep that night and was actually fed up of his dictatorial rule on me. I woke up with a headache the following morning and got ready for more of the headaches that day.

That was the day when my would-be *Bhabhi (would-be sister-in-law)* was supposed to visit our house and spend a day with us. No matter how Hitler-like my brother was, we loved each other to bits, and I was not very happy for him getting married. I was jealous of Roopam Bhabhi (my would-be sister-in-law) and thought that she would take my place in his life, and Monu Bhaiya ignored me like anything when she was around. She would take the front seat when the three of us went out in our car, and it was devastating for me to see someone else sit where I used to. Although Roopam Bhabhi was a great person, my jealousy and insecurity of losing my brother to her never made me feel close to her. Another reason for a headache that day was Roopam Bhabhi's presence in our lives.

When Bhabhi left for her place that night, I was scolded for not behaving properly and being a problem child. I tried to explain to my elders that I was no longer a child. I wanted to tell them that I even had a lover but bit my tongue for good. Monu Bhaiya insisted on me opting for nonmedical in another school, as my school was short of good math faculty as per his research. That meant a change of school for me for the next two years. Rahul wanted to choose medical, as he saw a doctor in himself (inspired by his dad), and our current school had the best biology teachers. I was shattered to think that we would not be in the same school now. I cried like hell that night and did not finish my dinner, but my Fauji (hindi word for a strict army man) dad was not affected by such tantrums, and my mother declared that I would not be given food for the subsequent day as well as she could never tolerate insults for the food.

Part 6

$\mathcal{I}$ loved all the subjects except math, physics, and chemistry. In other words, all I loved was English and physical education. I realized I would have been a lot better had I been studying humanities, but alas, my family members did not let me study my field of interest but theirs. I missed Mahtaab like anything and hated my new school. I began hating my life and wanted to run away. I found myself so lonely. So, there I was, in an alien land, trying to struggle my artistic brain with organic and inorganic, differentiation and integration, electricity and magnetism.

Practically all I enjoyed was literature and nothing else. I regretted following my family's dreams and not mine. Most of the youngsters believe that only sciences can bring them their share of success. But, in the due course, they forget that God blesses a chosen few with art. My dad thought that because my elder siblings could excel in the sciences, I would and I must do the same. My family members did not see the artist in Yashi, and this mistake on their part was enough for them to have a daughter who flunked in mathematics in Class XI finals. It was such a rude shock for the entire family.

My mom shouted at me at the top of her voice; Monu Bhaiya was all red in anger and terminated his communication with me. Ritu Didi was calling up after every half an hour to inquire what is next. I was fortunate enough that my dad was out of town that day as he had gone for his regiment's raising day celebrations. This fortune was not long lived, though.

He returned, drenched in the highest of his wrath that I had witnessed till that day. He entered my room where I was trying to cram some formulae, stared at me, and with his teeth clenched in disgust at watching a failure in front of him, yelled, "You black sheep of the family! Come here!" With that, he hit me hard on my head with his heavy, *strong* hand.

I lost count of the number of slaps I received after that. All I remember is that I had to meet Rahul the next day to earn his sympathies. (He was my only hope.) So, I covered my face with my hands and knelt down. The storm of bashes from my dad would not stop. I managed to turn my back and have the rest of the hits on it. I did not wish to have a black eye the next evening.

My phone rang, but I could not gather the guts to answer it. My mom yelled from the kitchen. The cooker's whistle and her voice got intermingled, but I could comprehend that she wanted me to answer the phone. I did as she directed.

"Hello, Yashi! Is that you?" It was an elegant female voice at the other end.

I answered, "Yes, this is! May I know who are you?"

The elegant, crisp voice started to show some signs of surprise. "Beta ji! This is Mrs. Malhotra, Rahul's mother. I heard about your result, so thought of calling you."

Another coin (another big one) dropped in my piggy bank of embarrassments. I was taken aback by her call and got ready for another round of scolding. Surprisingly, she empathized with me and asked me to focus on my compartment exam, which was scheduled the next week. She said she would be sending off Rahul to his aunt's place in Delhi to avoid any distractions.

I was disheartened but was brave enough to ask, "Can I meet him one last time before he leaves for Delhi?"

Part 7

Maybe she understood the desperation in the young girl's voice to meet the guy she loved and needed most in her hour of devastation. Yashi was a very sensitive human being, and she began to feel that all except her family members understood this fact. (Most of the adolescents find their harshest of enemies in the form of their parents; in my case, there were three distinct sets.)

Mama told me that she would be leaving for her club's meeting that afternoon, and I could meet him whenever I wanted. She regretted that she would not be able to see me that day. Rahul was supposed to leave for Delhi the next morning. I went to his home, again by taking a foolish risk of skipping classes. Love makes you an expert in taking risks.

There he was, my prince charming, feeling all sorry for my failure and not being happy for himself. (He scored 92 percent that year). He escorted me, as always, from the gate to the drawing room. He went to the kitchen to grab the Pepsi cans and the popcorn he'd made for me. In addition, he had brought a few packets of CRAX (ringed snacks, which I enjoy till date).

I had tears in my eyes. He sat next to me, held me by my shoulders, and wiped off the droplets falling down my eyes.

He said, "Yashi! My baby, no matter what, I am with you, now and forever."

He took me in the circumference of his strong arms. I realized that we were extremely close. I could smell his cologne, and my soft cheeks could feel his thorny, fresh, young bearded face. The sofa on which both of us were sitting, which had been big enough to handle both of us each of the previous times we couched on it for casual movies or chemistry lectures, suddenly seemed too small. Maybe we grew up a little too much.

He whispered in my ear, "I wish to carry the snacks to my bed, along with you."

I nodded, closed my eyes and smiled.

He carried me in his arms and, like a graceful gentleman, put me down on his bed. He sat next to me and was playing with my hair. I felt him staring at me with an immense amount of love and passion. I was feeling shy, even to look at him straight in his lovely eyes.

Ding dong. The culprit was the doorbell.

Part 8

It was Rahul's dad; he needed some papers from home. Rahul went ahead to open the door. Uncle didn't enter Rahul's room but inquired about the magenta-colored Miss India bike. Rahul told him that it was a friend's who was over to *study*. His dad was in a hurry, so he left. After he was gone, it was time for me to depart. We kissed each other good-bye and smiled at what was almost accomplished. He wished me luck and motivated me to study hard for my compartment exam.

The exam happened, and I just passed it. I found Grade XII curriculum easier than grade XI. I managed to pass all my exams in monthly tests and half yearly. The real acid test to sail through boards was yet to come. Rahul and I decided that we would be focusing on our studies and not on each other until after the final exams. I gathered myself and got back on track. I studied very hard, day and night. My parents were finally satisfied with my performance. In the meantime, Monu Bhaiya's wedding was in February. I could not enjoy it, because of my upcoming final exams in March.

When the exams were finished, we waited keenly for the results. I was hoping not to flunk this time. My dreams came true. I scored 70.4 percent and was thrilled about it. Rahul got 95 percent and was among the city toppers in CBSE (Central Board of Secondary Education). I was very happy for him, as well as myself. My parents and siblings were cool about my performance. Then I began to believe that my failure in Class XI was important for my family to lower their expectations.

Then came the time for CET (Common Engineering Test) and PMT (Pre Medical Test) exams. I never wanted to be an engineer ever in my life but still appeared for the exams. Rahul always wanted to be a doctor. Even though there were only five seats in the general category for MBBS (Bachelor in Medicine and Bachelor in Surgery) in CMC (Christian Medical College) and seven in DMC (Dayanand Medical College), Rahul got admission in both of the colleges. He opted for DMC, as it was closer to his place.

As far as my competition results were concerned, my rank was nowhere near to where I could get through in computer engineering or electronics, even with the defense quota. So, my brother decided that I would be joining BCA (bachelor of computer applications) in a local college in Ludhiana (Punjab). I was happy with the decision, because computers fascinated me, and I knew I would not be required to study high-level math, physics, or chemistry. Plus, Rahul and I would be in the same city.

The college days began with full enthusiasm and zeal. I became interested in education once again. My hobbies revived again. I was the star poetess of the college again. By the second year's end, I was offered the office of the editor of the English section of the college magazine. I got back in my form, and to add to the happiness, my nephew was born. Ritu Didi was a mother, and I was an aunt. It was so thrilling, as I was finally elder to someone in the family. The baby was named Raghav, and my mom flew all the way to the UK to help my sister at the time when she needed her. I was dying to see Raghav. My happiness knew no boundaries.

On the other hand, Monu Bhaiya and Roopam Bhabhi were getting to know each other. Bhabhi was a perfect daughter-in-law that most families would dream of, but I could somehow not let go of my jealousy and could not share my brother with her. I yelled at her in every possible situation. I felt like a bitch sometimes but just could not help it. Bhabhi never uttered a word in front of me, and she never complained. Gradually, I accepted her, and now she is my best pal and a role model.

Rahul was working hard on his MBBS, studying anatomy, physiology, pathology, psychology, gynecology, and what not. We spent less time together, owing to our careers. I was in the third year of my graduation now and started preparing for my MCA (Master of Computer Application) entrance. This time, I prepared with all my heart and soul in it. I knew that if I had to have my way in terms of my marriage, I had to study hard and secure a good job. Otherwise, no member of my family would agree for a love marriage. Monu Bhaiya and Ritu Didi both had undergone the tedious process of an arranged marriage. They were too busy to fall in love.

Mama was in touch with me consistently, and her trust in me strengthened over the years. She admitted in front of me that as soon as Rahul secured his admission in his masters from a good college (he was a bright student, so that time was not very far away), she and uncle would visit my place and ask for my hand. Over the years of diligence in our fields of academia, Rahul and I realized that even if we did not talk for days together, our love only strengthened and did not diminish. My MCA entrance exam went off amazingly, and I topped the state of Punjab. I could pick and choose the college I wanted. I finally got admission to the University of my choice and proceeded one step closer toward my personal and professional aim.

Part 9

$\mathcal{I}$ clearly remember that it was the final year of my masters. All my classmates were gearing up for the upcoming placements. Infosys, Wipro, TCS, TechM, Accenture, and several other companies were visiting our campus. I was aiming for Infosys, as it was the dream company for most of the students. In addition, not many people were satisfying the eligibility criteria for the company. I was among the fortunate ones who met Infy's benchmarks. Its Mysore campus was a dream destination. Infosys was the first company visiting us that year.

Rahul was in internship that year and became a very busy man. It was for the first time that we could not speak much for one full week. He knew I was busy with my studies and job placement exams, and he was learning new things every day and treating people to the best of his capabilities in ER.

The preplacement talk for Infosys was amazing. I so much yearned to be a part of it. The exam happened, and by the afternoon, results for the written test were out. My family members were in touch with me until my phone's battery died. I was the only one from MCA, apart from forty students from B.Tech., who passed the written part. The top students in my class were showing signs of immense confusion, jealousy and disgust. They still managed the fake smiles and wished me good luck for the interview, although they silently prayed that I should not get selected. Somehow, God did not pay any heed to their mean prayers, and I sailed through as a star by being the first one to be placed with Infosys. It was an amazing feeling; it made me realize my hidden potential, as well as the true colors of many of my classmates. The only classmates who were genuinely happy were my friends Nidhi Kapoor, Vishakha and Harry. Nidhi, Vishakha and Harry were always fun to be with.

The next morning was a day full of congratulations and celebrations. Monu Bhaiya and Bhabhi travelled all the way from Ludhiana to Patiala (where I studied) to pick me up. I saw the glitter in the eyes of all my family members and wished to see the same in Rahul's eyes. I had not told him about my placement yet. Moreover, he was on night duty. I called him up in the afternoon and asked about his plans. I told him that I was in Patiala, because I had *not* cleared my test with Infy. He consoled me and wished me luck for the next exam. I somehow hid my happiness and laughter. I wanted to give him a surprise. He was on leave that day and was supposed to spend the rest of his day at home.

I told my dad that I wished to meet some of my friends that evening and throw a party for them. My dad was elated and handed me about five thousand rupees (Indian Currency INR) to enjoy my achievement. In addition, he asked Bhaiya to lend me his car for that evening. This happened for the first time in my life that no one in my family sulked on knowing the fact that I would be late that evening. My family was proud of me. My dream of having a great career and an even greater man was soon to come true.

I went in my brother's posh car to meet Rahul. I planned a great surprise for him. I carried a large bunch of roses and his favorite chocolates (Ferrero Rochers), and DVD of our favorite movie (*Titanic*). I knew he would be the happiest man to have a well settled and employed girl.

With my heart beating and each beat saying his name aloud, I rushed to his home. I was dressed up in a beautiful black dress. I carried all his presents and, for the first time, did not ring the doorbell. I walked straight in. I noticed that Uncle and Mama weren't home. I loved Mama for having a very active social life. It gave us all the quality time we needed.

I was lucky that the door was open. I walked in, spreading the fragrance of my Polo perfume all over the place. I carried myself forward with my silent footsteps toward his room. What I saw next was really uncalled for. I saw Rahul in his boxers, lying down on his bed with a few thick medical books opened. Lying next to him was Alka (my best friend and Rahul's classmate in DMC).

The bunch of roses fell off my hand. The chocolate box hit the wall. They probably heard that. My heart skipped I don't know how many beats. My tears would not stop. I never imagined seeing my man with my best friend in his bed with no clothes on him. It was a bigger failure for me that my Class XI compartment. Rahul jumped out of his bed. Alka sat up straight. I threw the gifts all over the place and sobbed and sobbed.

Part 10

$\mathscr{I}$ sat in the drawing room on the couch. I was genuinely hurt by what I saw. Alka came out of the room and sat next to me. She asked me the reason behind my behavior. I was very angry and chose not to respond; I found solace in my tears and continued the process of weeping.

Alka asked me, "Yashi, What is wrong with you? Why are you overreacting?"

I answered, "Let him come in here too; only then will I utter a word."

Rahul came and sat in front of me on the carpet. He was clothed then. He held my hand and asked, "Why are you crying?"

I lost my temper and yelled at him, "What would you do if you saw me in my bed in my bare essentials with Dr. Abhineet, your friend?"

Rahul frowned and said, "Darling! Did you notice something on my body?"

I answered, "No, you were not naked in front of me, right? Alka must have noticed. By the way, what is it?"

He took off his shirt and showed me his back. It had bruises, and I could not interpret the same.

I asked him, "What is it?"

Rahul said, I got this weird infection from one of my patients and did not wish to bother you at all as you were busy with your placements. This was hurting me a lot, as it is a very painful skin infection."

My next question was, "Why was Alka here when you were not clothed?"

He said, "Alka came here to study, as we have our AIIMS entrance in another ten months. She wanted to have a look at my infection, just on a professional ground. Please, Lips, please trust me. Do you think Mahtaab can ever betray you?"

Every cell of my body wanted to answer in negative. I noticed Mahtaab had tears in his eyes. I felt that tears just did not suit him. Alka came forward and swore on her parents that she would never carry such feelings for Rahul.

She said, "Yashi! I know what this man means to you, and by the way, I want to tell you that Dr. Abhineet and I are getting engaged soon. He proposed to me last week. I wanted you to get a placement and then we thought of throwing a party for you guys. Please, Yashi, don't think that your guy is wrong, as I was just trying to analyze his skin disease and nothing else. There would not be a greater sin for anyone than trying to split you guys up. Plus, I am your best friend, and how could you even imagine that we would screw up your life?"

Then it was Rahul's turn to speak. "Darling! You are the only person I love in this world, next to my family. Please never think that I would betray you, that too for another girl. We have been together for the past nine years now, and the day after I clear the AIIMS (All India Institute of Medical Sciences) exam my family will come and seek your alliance for me. I plan to live my life with you, Sweety! I plan to have children with you, and I wish to grow old with you, lose my teeth, and share the dentures with you. Above all, I wish I die ahead of you in your arms. I cannot ask for more than that from God. You know how much I believe in Mata ji (Durga Mata, the mother goddess). I swear on her that you are the only one for me."

What emotional girl would not believe such explanations? I ended up feeling guilty to even doubt my love. I apologized and told all to drop the topic. I told them both the news about my placement. Alka sat there for a while and then left Rahul and I alone. Rahul congratulated me and kissed me on my forehead for the first time. Since we grew up together, we never felt the desire to be physically very close to each other, as we had other ways to express our love, like watching *Titanic* together, making popcorn and Maggi noodles for each other, serving Pepsi on the rocks, and talking for hours together. We gathered the chocolates from the ground and ate them. Rahul was very happy and *decently dressed*.

It was time for me to go home. Rahul came out to see me off and was impressed to see me in my brother's Honda. He knew I was very fond of posh cars. My brother gave me a call as I stood outside my guy's home. Bhaiya was sounding panicky. "Yashi! Please visit DMC soon."

I asked him, "Bhai! What is wrong?"

He said, "Dear, your Bhabhi has been taken there." Then he disconnected the phone.

Bhabhi was eight months pregnant and was instructed not to travel, but she did the previous day to pick me up from Patiala. I told Rahul what had happened. Rahul grabbed his ID card, and we hopped in my car and rushed to DMC. I saw my family really tensed out there.

For the first time in my life, I realized how important my Bhabhi was for my family and my brother. Their first child was expected. Rahul went straight inside the ER. He came out after ten minutes, held my hand in front of the entire family, and announced, "Bhabhi has faced some complications, and she needs to be operated on immediately. Bhaiya, I will take care of the formalities. Please relax, and we will do our best."

More than the feeling of love, it was the feeling of respect I had for him at that moment. I prayed with all my heart that my Bhabhi and the child should be okay. The celebration time was turning into a tense time. I saw him putting on his mask and gazing at me with hopeful eyes. They took Roopam Bhabhi to the operating room. We were waiting outside, and all of us sang our most honest prayers.

It was after about what seemed ages to us and two hours by the clock that the senior gynecologist came out.

Part 11

He said with a grin on his face, "Mr. Manish (my brother's name), were you prepared for twins?"

My Bhaiya said, "What, Doctor? Is my wife OK?"

"She is out of danger and has given birth to healthy twins," the doctor said. "It was a miracle that we could save all of them. One of the babies was very serious and had caught pneumonia. Now all are perfectly fine!"

Suddenly, I asked, "Boy or girl? I mean, boys or girls or whatever?"

The doctor smiled and answered, "One boy and one girl. The family is completed in one go. Well done, young man!"

My brother blushed, and one by one we all went to catch the glimpse of babies. They were so beautifully cute. We named them Radhika and Uday. I was extremely elated. Rahul walked out of the labor room and congratulated all of us.

My dad asked me, "Who is he? How do you know him?"

I replied, "Dad, this is my classmate Dr. Rahul, an internee in DMC and a very bright doctor."

Dad smiled and thanked Rahul for his proactive response in Bhabhi's case. It was so much fun to have twins. Life was all cool now.

The babies were cute and silly at the same time. It was the year of babies for us. Next, it was Ritu Didi's turn to have a baby girl named Ambika, and my parents went to the UK to support her. I thought Rahul and I would give the old couple a break for at least six years. Ideally, in the next few years, Rahul should be joining his MS in AIIMS. He was very well prepared, and we were just awaiting the entrance. We planned to get engaged after he cleared his AIIMS exam. Then we thought of getting married after three years, when Rahul would be in the final year of his MS (Masters in Surgery). Babies would wait for a while.

It was the fall of that year when Ritu Didi and Jiju planned to visit India with both the children. I finished with my masters and moved to New Delhi for my six-month industrial training. It was a great learning experience. I used to visit Ludhiana every weekend. Twice a month I met Rahul, and we planned our future. By that time, Mama told Rahul's dad about me, and then I was universally accepted as a very intelligent daughter-in-law of the family. After all, Infosys was a company all the oldies in India knew and bragged about it if their kids worked there.

We had a lot of fun when Didi was here. It was a family reunion. Didi got three NRI alliances for me, and I shared with her that I didn't wish to settle abroad. I gave her reasons like I was against brain drain and what not. She was convinced, and after about a month of fun and frolic in India, she left to go back to the UK. She wished me good luck for Infosys and admitted that the entire family was proud of me, at last.

It was one of the sought after weekends in winters that one of my friends from Delhi came to visit me. Her name was Tanu. She knew about Rahul's presence in my life and was very keen on meeting him. I used to brag about his lovely eyes in front of all my friends. I fixed up a meeting for Tanu, Rahul, and myself.

Tanu was a flirty girl. Our ground rules never matched. She was my roommate and was a very hip person. She used to booze hard, go out at night, and dance like a stripper. She had all the fun in her life that I never had. She changed her guys like her dresses. They sponsored her meals, dresses, and whatnot. Despite of all this, we shared a strong bond. The dissimilarities in terms of ground rules were there, for sure. But there was something that made us good friends. I do not know what it was. Maybe, secretly, I wanted to have the fun she had as well.

So, there we were at Colonel's Cabin, a famous pub in Ludhiana. I was scared to death to visit a pub and took a promise from Tanu that she would exercise controlled drinking. What happened next came as a surprise.

Part 12

$\mathscr{T}$anu ordered one large Smirnoff for herself, and Rahul and I ordered a pitcher of Pepsi. Once she was done with her drinking, we all went to the dance floor. I saw the door of the pub open, and someone entered. Since all of us were busy dancing, I didn't pay much attention. Rahul and I were in a close, cuddly dance posture and were enjoying the music. Tanu, as expected, had already fetched herself a hunky man for company. I never understood how she did it with such tremendous ease. Her extreme good looks were definitely an asset for her in this regard. I never wanted to learn the art of flirting from her, as I was very serious with Rahul. When Rahul was with me, I never felt the need of any other person in my life (of course, family is an altogether different category).

I felt a tap at my back. It was a familiar touch. I turned back, and in the disco lights, I saw an angry face of Monu Bhaiya. I felt myself being held by the hand and dragged outside the pub. Rahul, the courageous, followed me. Tanu was high on vodka and continued her stripper girl dance. Bhaiya took Rahul and me to his car, opened the doors by his remote, and instructed us to get in. He drove away. After ten minutes of a silent and violent drive, he parked the car to the left of the road, turned on the hazard lights, pulled up the hand brakes, and after putting the car in neutral, gave me a frosty-nosed stare.

"This is the same doctor who held your hand the other day in front of all of us, right?" he asked.

I realized it was time for me to speak up. I said, "Yes, Bhaiya."

"Since when has this crap been happening? Be honest with me."

I chose to remain silent. Bhaiya looked up to him in the backseat and inquired of Rahul, "Where do you live?"

Rahul answered, "Bhaiya! #232, Block C, Sarabha Nagar."

Bhaiya asked him, "Are your parents aware?"

Rahul answered in affirmative.

I could feel that Bhaiya was badly hurt. With trembling lips, I asked him, "What brought you there, Bhai?"

Bhaiya clenched his teeth and answered, "None of your business!"

Bhaiya drove back to Colonel's Cabin, dropped Rahul there, and there was Tanu, standing outside, red in anger, waiting for us. Bhaiya told me to give her my car keys and come home in that. I did not wish that Bhai create a scene in front of her but did not have the guts to vent out after the ordeal that we had faced. Rahul stood there, and Tanu followed our car as she wasn't sure of the routes in Ludhiana. I was scared to death. What if Bhaiya would go home and announce what he had just seen! I would be a dead duck. Dad would shoot me, and Mom would shout at me. Maybe Bhai read my mind.

He said, "When and where is your joining with Infy expected?"

"I don't know, Bhaiya. Maybe in late November this year. It will be Mysore, for sure," I answered.

"I want you to concentrate on your job Beta, as this is the age when you can learn. Everyone has to get married. I understand that you must have been lonely in your life, as all of us were busy in establishing my business empire so that we could give you and the other kids a comfortable life. Dad would really be hurt if he found out what I saw tonight. There is almost a double generation gap between you and Mom and Dad, so I understand why you went astray. Moreover, I don't have any hard feelings for that doctor of yours, but please consider all the options before you make a final decision. I don't want you to be carried away by your emotions and make a hasty decision."

"What do you feel I should do, Bhaiya?" I said to calm down things a bit.

"He needs to establish himself before he can think about you, and you should also have a wider exposure. Let me speak to his parents tomorrow first," my brother said.

I heard what Bhai had just said and got really scared, as it was a very big deal for me to be caught like that.

"Bhaiya, would you support me if he gets selected in AIIMS. You know, he is preparing really well for his upcoming MS entrance exam."

"I could see that, Yashi! The kind of preparation that young man had for his exam."

"Please, Bhaiya, he is a great guy and I wish to marry him and no one else."

We reached home. Bhaiya did not utter a word in front of the family. Tanu was drunk, so she went straight to my room and slept. Fortunately, she did not create a scene in front of my folks. Maybe it was her stamina of boozing that kept her going.

The next morning, Tanu had to leave for Delhi, and I was told to stay back, as per my brother's instructions. Now my Bhabhi also knew about the doctor in my life. They decided to meet his parents and took me along the next evening. I was told to arrange a meeting. Rahul and I were badly tensed, as it was the testing time for us and our love. We decided not to lie about anything. I got dressed up for what was the first formal family meeting. Dad and Mom had no clue about anything that was going on. Rahul's family invited us for dinner. His mom was a great cook, and I had absolutely no doubts that she would convince Bhai and Bhabhi. After all, if Bhaiya would agree, everyone else automatically would be convinced, as he had amazing articulation and negotiation skills. He was an expert in making any situation a win-win for him. So, secretly, I was counting on him for his approval. Indian youth seek approval for anything and everything that has to be done. I sometimes feel that we forget to follow our heart in seeking permission.

We went to their home. Mama had decorated it beautifully, and we were given a very warm greeting. The twins were toddlers then and were playing with things here and there. Bhabhi had to follow them everywhere, as they had become experts in breaking things. They were extremely naughty and made the tension in the environment diluted.

Then came the real question by Bhaiya, "Uncle, I am a very straightforward person. So, I would like to ask you about your views on Yashi's and Rahul's relationship. I was told that both of you know about it."

His dad said, "Mr. Joshi, I would want to say that we really like Yashi, and we want her to be a part of this family. Rahul and Yashi make a great couple, and we do not have any demands except that Rahul has to appear for his AIIMS entrance next month, and his result will be out in a week. We can have the engagement ceremony after that."

Mama said, "She is a girl who is my son's life, and since both the kids will be well settled soon, we should be happy in whatever they are happy with."

It was my brother's turn to speak. "Rahul, if you clear your AIIMS entrance, only then this marriage can happen, as in our family, education is very important. I would be able to convince my dad only if you get admitted in MS. For your knowledge, Yashi is already getting offers of marriage from the biggest of industrialists, as well as very well educated NRI (Non Resident Indians). But trust me; I will manage everything if you get through in your exam. Last but not the least, I like you as a person and a professional, as you played a vital role in handling my wife's emergency."

Rahul was trying to smile when Bhabhi said, "She would be working with Infosys, and they do not have a DC (Development Centre) in Delhi. So, how will we resolve that issue?"

There was pin-drop silence for a while. None of us had thought about it before. Rahul was the only child of his parents. He had to be at a reachable distance from his home. His dad had a great practice in Ludhiana.

Everyone looked confused.

Part 13

I said, "Rahul might want to get settled in Chandigarh, as Infy has a DC in Chandigarh, and we have PGI, another leading medical college there as well." Bhabhi was satisfied with the answer.

His dad said, "I like you family's straightforwardness. We certainly do not have any problem with them settling in Chandigarh. At least it is nearer to Ludhiana than Delhi."

Rahul smiled and agreed to the proposal. So, everything was set. All of us were sure that this marriage would happen.

After our family meeting, Rahul didn't talk much to me, as he had better reasons to clear the exam now. I didn't disturb him either. It was my birthday the next week, and I decided to celebrate it in Delhi with Tanu and other friends. I just informed him of the same. My treat was going on in CP when I saw Rahul entering with a bunch of red roses. He was dressed to kill in his navy blue suit. Oh! I felt I fell in love with him once again.

He hugged me and said, "Two more weeks to go, Lips. I will be staying at my aunt's place tonight, and I have to visit AIIMS tomorrow to submit some documents. I wanted to give you a surprise and so I asked Tanu where you guys would be celebrating. So, here I am. I thank my pretty saali for this." He winked at Tanu in a friendly manner.

Tanu, as expected, was high on her Smirnoff. We sat and all of us were talking. Tanu said, "Dr. Saab! This girl praises about your eyes a lot. What is the color of your pair, if I may ask?" I was taken aback at the question, as it was inappropriate.

Rahul answered the drunken woman by removing his rimless specs and flaunting his eyes, "Please help yourself by judging the color yourself."

The flirt in both of them came out, and they giggled. Suddenly, I felt jealous as never before. Rahul probably didn't even realize that he had hurt me. I paid the bill and walked out of the restaurant.

Rahul followed me, and with an innocent expression on his face, he asked me, "Can I not joke with anyone? I am all yours, but I don't understand why I have to prove it again and again."

I had tears rolling down my face, and I was extremely angry at him. I said, "That's what. You never understand. You know what your eyes mean to me, and you were flaunting it just like that. I feel possessive about you, and I don't wish to share you with anyone else. I am feeling miserable, Rahul."

Rahul pointed out to a locket of Mata ji in the chain I was wearing. He said, "I will try my best never to disappoint you. Please forgive me one last time."

Then we displayed extreme emotions. I had never been angry with him to this extent. In a fit of rage, I said what I should never have, "Rahul! You are dead to me." And then I rushed home.

Rahul called me later that night and said, "Lips! I am leaving for Ludhiana tomorrow. I am sorry for the behavior that you considered inappropriate, but, Babes, please never say things the burden of which you cannot carry for the rest of your life." I apologized and wished him a happy journey, as I did not want to disturb or distract him in his preparations for his (rather our) exam.

Two weeks later, the big day arrived. We planned that I would be there waiting for him outside AIIMS. It must be mentioned that Rahul was an extremely punctual fellow. I was worried that I would have to be ready in time for my wedding, or else he'd eat my head up. He hated to arrive anywhere late or have others arrive late. His exam was scheduled at the one o'clock to three o'clock time slot. He was supposed to reach AIIMS main gate by eleven o'clock that morning. I had taken a day off and got my joining date with Infosys, two months later for Nov 12th, 2007. Rahul was elated to know that. It meant, in any case, we would be engaged in the coming two months, before I left for Mysore (a town in South India with the biggest training facility in the world owned by Infosys). Everything was so settled.

I was reciting Durga Chalisa (prayer chants of the Hindu Mother Goddess) as I waited for him there, holding my mobile phone. The last message I received from him was at eight o'clock that morning. It said, "Reached Kurukshetra, Darling! Two more hours, and I will be there. It's a little foggy here, but don't worry, Chimpu is driving really well."

I replied, "Waiting for you desperately. Will Reach AIIMS by 10:30. Love you to bits, honeybunch."

Alka and Abhineet had already reached and met me at the gate. They were engaged then and came in the train as they had to study on their way. I wished them luck. Looking tensed, they said, "We really know, from the bottom of our hearts, that Rahul is going to make it. We are here just for an experience, but Rahul will definitely do it. So, just chill." They continued digging their noses in their large books.

The thoughts of past and present were crossing my mind. I was imagining and planning the upcoming evening with Chimpu and Rahul. Chimpu was Rahul's first cousin, who was always treated as the real sibling in his house. He was a sweetheart in all respects. He lovingly addressed me as "Bhaabhoo."

The clock struck 12:45 p.m. Abhineet and Alka, along with about hundred others went inside the examination hall. Rahul was late. I was trying his phone desperately, but every time it was a lady in a happy tone telling me that the number was "unreachable." I was pissed off to the max. I thought that he must have entered from the other gate. At the same time, I was worried for his safety. I was in my thought hurricane that my phone buzzed. It was Mama calling.

I answered the phone, "Namaste (Indian traditional greeting), Mama. Rahul isn't here yet. Do you have any information?"

Mama sounded visibly upset and asked, "Dear! Are you alone out there, or is someone there with you?"

"Mama! What happened? I am waiting for him here, and you know he is already late."

"Beta ji! Please go home, as Rahul entered the hall from the other gate and told me to tell you. Call me when you reach home," she explained.

"Mama, he cannot do it. He promised me he would see me first, and then he would appear for the exam."

"Beta ji! He tried your phone, but it was busy all the time. He was running late for the exam, and so he told me to tell you."

"Okay, Mama, I'll call you when I reach home," I said.

I was frowning all through my drive back home. I did not like the way he treated me. I was angry at Chimpu's driving as well, but at the same time, I wanted him to clear the exam so that we could proceed further in life. I reached home and called up Mama. I could hear weird noises in the background. Mama asked me if someone else was around me. I answered that just my maid was there.

Mama spoke what was really not expected. "Beta ji! Rahul and Chimpu met with an accident near Karnal. A truck hit their Zen. I am sorry I lied to you, but I had to send you home somehow. Beta ji! His dad and chachu (uncle) have left for Karnal and are on their way back." Then, for the first time, I heard Mama sobbing.

I asked, "Mama, when did this happen?"

"Around eight forty this morning, beta, and we found out about fifteen minutes later."

It was already three o'clock, and I disconnected the phone. I could not think for the next few hours. I wanted to go to Ludhiana but could not move. I was taken to the hospital, as I had collapsed. At the same AIIMS where I wished to see him in a lab coat and his stethoscope, I was being treated by a bunch of strange doctors.

They said nothing was wrong with me. Tanu, Abhineet, and Alka were with me. All were upset at knowing that Rahul could not make it. More than my wedding, I wanted him to survive that mishap.

I was lying down like a dead body on my bed. Alka, Abhineet, and Tanu surrounded me. "Dr. Gagan calling."

She was one of our common friends and was a dentist at Christian Dental College. She was a very studious and bright dentist and a great friend. She had always been an integral part of my life as a darling friend.

Rahul and Chimpu were admitted to DMC. Gagan told me that Chimpu was declared dead on arrival. Rahul suffered severe head injuries and was in a coma. I was so shocked that I could not even cry. Yashi, who was known as the weeping beauty, had no tears at all. I was shell-shocked and too overwhelmed to react.

Alka took the phone from my hand and told Gagan to keep us informed. It was a cold, chilly night in late winter. I finally got up at 12:45 a.m. to use the restroom. I was inside when I heard my phone buzzing. I rushed outside quickly, and it was Gagan. I picked up the phone. All I could hear were screams and noises. Gagan was sobbing and was not speaking at all. I shouted at Gagan, "Please hurry up and let me know. How is he? How is my green eyes? How is my Mahtaab?"

There was a long silence from the other end, and following the silence were Gagan's words, "Yashi, I am sorry. He could not be saved. He is gone."

I screamed at the top of my voice. My eleven years of relationship was snatched in a split second by the cruel hands of destiny. I was a mere spectator in my life's drama. I could not think, could not speak, and could not cry, and because of my health, I was not in a condition to travel to Ludhiana.

I wanted to speak to Mama. "How are you, Mama?" I asked.

"How can I be, Yashi! My world is shattered. His dad has gone to get the body."

I yelled at her, "For heaven's sake, Mama! He has a name. He is not a body. He is Yashi's Mahtaab."

Mama hung up the phone. Though my friends were there, they failed to comfort me. Gagan called up the next morning and told me that Rahul and Chimpu were being taken for cremation. It was then that I cried. I never imagined him being burnt. He hated fire, I remembered. I told Alka to convey this to Mama, but she understood that I was bound to react this way.

All she said was, "Babes! All of us understand what you are going through, but you should also understand that no matter what, your depression and grief can never match his parents' levels of despair. They have lost their only child. It sunk in me that whatever Alka was saying was correct and that I had two options there on. One was to kill myself and be free from every misery, and the second one was to live my life and fight a battle every day from there on.

I never imagined my life without him. He was cremated. It was only after a week I was discharged from the hospital. Then Abhineet, Alka, and I went to Rahul's house in Ludhiana—same house, same Parents, but many differences. I entered the drawing room, and the picture of me being carried up in a bridal *lehnga* to his room in his arms was shattered to bits by his life-sized poster in the same navy blue suit that he'd worn for my birthday a few days back behind a garland of red roses. I felt his green eyes piercing every cell of my body.

I regretted my words, "Rahul! You are dead for me!" more than anything else in my life.

Mama was inconsolable, but she was a lady of immense strength. She asked me to be bold and know that he was just right there besides us.

I wanted to believe her, but I could not.

ANOTHER WALK OF LIFE

Part 14

Tears welled up in my eyes. So many of them that the outburst could not be controlled anymore, and they found their way down on my cheeks and ended on the bunch of greeting cards he gave me over the years that I was holding, drop by drop. It was very hard for me to digest that he was gone, and I would not see him ever again.

I tried to smell the ink on the card that said, "I love you eternally, this life and many more . . ." and longed for a faint trace of his fragrance. As always, I failed. He had been gone almost six months. My training with Infosys, Mysore was nearing completion, and like most of my batch mates, I had applied for a week-long leave to visit my native place, Ludhiana. Lemy, my roomie in Mysore entered the room and saw me crying.

"Oh Yashi! Not again," she said. "It won't work this way. You have to move on."

I tried to wipe off my tears and manage a fake smile and said, "Ya, Lemy, I understand, but grieving is a part of the whole process of moving on. Isn't it?"

She very wisely decided not to take the argument further and went out of the room. We were through with our comprehensive exam and were scheduled to relocate to Bangalore for our ILI sessions, as there was some corporate event coming up in Mysore.

The ILI (Infosys Leadership Institute) sessions went off amazingly well, and the final postings came. I got Hyderabad DC as my location. All my batch mates were thrilled with the idea of starting the real job now. In our Volvos, we marched toward our destination, and Infosys Hyderabad's ECC (Employee Care Center, these are some of the best-in-class facilities we had) awaited us. Once the formal reporting to human resources in Hyderabad was over, I took a flight to Delhi from Hyderabad's Shamsabad Airport.

As I landed, many memories involving the city drooled over my head. The time when I stood outside AIIMS waiting for him on that fateful day flashed right in front of me as my cab crossed the AIIMS complex on my way to the railway station. I actually saw a part of me waiting for him then. I guess that part would never move on and would continue to analyze the tragedy that had been thrown in my face. These thoughts kept me engaged as we reached the Railway station.

"250 rupees, madam!" the cab driver said.

I realized the difference between Dad's money and my own hard-earned money, as it pinched me a lot to spare my 250 bucks to that smelly cab driver with stained teeth and a perverted smile. He helped me with my luggage and went off. I was lost in thought again when I realized that about ten coolies were surrounding me. I felt suffocated and shooed them away. I managed my luggage somehow, reached the platform, and sat there waiting for Shatabdi. The huge rush suffocated me even more. I think it was not the crowd that made me uncomfortable but my thoughts that were suffocating not only my respiratory system but my view as well. Again, I had tears in my eyes as I remembered the journey back home with Alka and Abhineet after Rahul's death. It was in a Shatabdi as well.

I tried to shrug off my thoughts, as I did not want to be an object of public curiosity. I found my seat and settled down. Next to me was a stupid man who was talking very loudly on his phone, and it was an irritating gesture for me. After he was done with his loud and baseless blabbering, he played some Punjabi songs. It irritated me to such a level that I took out my iPod and stuck up the earphones and had to compulsorily listen to all the sad songs that were my hot choice after his death.

"Awaarapan Banjaarapan" by KK made me a little upset. All the heights of gloom were crossed when I heard the next song on the list, "Chitthi na koi Sandesh." Then it didn't bother me if my sobs were heard by about ten people in the train. I wished that they would mind their own business. But as is the norm in this country, people did not, and the stupid man next to me muted his Punjabi songs and asked me, "Madam! Are you all right?"

I answered, "Oh yes! Please don't worry and thanks for asking"

He didn't bother to inquire further. I declined offers for refreshments in Shatabdi over and over again to the point that the refreshment guy didn't bother to ask me anymore. He must have thought that I was fasting.

I felt asleep for a while during the train journey as I heard hustle bustle suddenly when my iPod's charge was gone. The train was about to reach Ludhiana Junction. I gathered my luggage and peeped outside the window to see who had come to pick me up. I was glad to see Bhaiya and Bhabhi on the platform.

The train halted. Bhaiya took my luggage, and I got down. I was elated to meet the children (Uday and Radhika) after what seemed like ages, but only three months had gone by on the calendar. We marched toward home. Dad and Mom were eagerly waiting on the terrace, and I felt special. For a little while, I got rid of Mahtaab's thoughts in the whole process of family reunion. Bhabhi had prepared Rajmaah-Chawal (Red beans and Basmati rice) for me that evening, as it was my favorite dish. After about two hours of chitchat and sharing of experiences I had in Mysore, I left for my room. Two days later was Rahul's birthday, and I was thinking of all the previous birthdays we had celebrated together. These thoughts were heavy enough to put my tired body on rest, and I didn't realize when sleep conquered me.

Part 15

$\mathcal{I}$ slept until eleven o'clock the next morning. It was a very well-deserved sleep after the fast-track training in Mysore and tight schedules in Bangalore. I loved getting up late, and it was such a good feeling to hop around the house all day without caring for a bath. I had *aloo paranthaas (Indian stuffed bread served in breakfast)* for brunch and relished the taste that I had almost forgotten staying in the south. Mom and Bhabhi left no stone unturned to feed me till I was so full that I almost cried as I pleaded for no more *paranthaas*.

After the lovely brunch, it was time for me to play with the kids. They had started mumbling meaningful words by then, which were amusing for me to comprehend. "Toy, toy . . . Bua, I banna toy." Uday said these words, and I remembered that I still hadn't handed out presents that I had brought for all my family members. I got Mysore silk sarees for my mom, Bhabhi, and sis; a tie for my dad; and a shirt for Bhaiya and Jiju. It was a brilliant feeling as I handed over the gifts to them. The kids looked up longingly, and it was then that I realized I forgot to bring anything for them. Fortunately, I had four crackle chocolates in my handbag, which came to the rescue. They were elated to the max and resumed their running all over the place.

I went back to my room after I'd distributed the gifts and stared at the walls blankly. In fact, I was turning good at this staring thing. It occurred to me that it was his twenty-fourth birthday the next day. I decided that even if he wasn't with me physically, I would still celebrate the day. And then I thought about how it must be even more difficult for his parents to survive through his first birthday without him. Amidst the thought hurricane, I took a nap, and when I woke up, it was already six o'clock the following morning.

I got up and headed toward the bathroom to have a quick shower. After the shower, I was getting ready when I heard a knock at my door. It was Alka; she had come to visit me and knew I would be planning something for Rahul's family on his birthday. She greeted me with a huge hug and asked me, "How have you been, Yashi!? How do you plan to celebrate the day?"

I smiled and answered, "I wish to have my share of his birthday cake and some chocolates with some Chinese food. What is your pick?"

Alka said, "It seems like a great idea. I am sure he would love it from up above the skies." Her statement made me realize that I wouldn't see him this time on his day. But this thought didn't deter me.

As I was about to leave for the market, Bhabhi asked me where was I going. I decided to tell her the whole thing, as it was very difficult for me to lie about him. The liar in me was gone with him, I think. She had tears in her eyes and said, "All the best dear! I am with you."

I told Alka that in my family only Bhaiya and Bhabhi knew about him and his death. We just didn't get a chance to discuss it with our parents. Once he died, I asked Bhaiya not to disclose it in front of Dad, as he could not see me sad. There was one more reason that I did not want to answer a million questions that would have followed if they found out about my relationship. Moreover, there was no need for me to share the trauma I was going through with them.

Alka and I went to Sindhi's (a renowned bakery in India) and ordered his favorite black forest cake with additional chocolate on it. He ordered one extra pack of chocolate, as I always ate most of those. The man at the bakery said, "You can pick it up at eleven o'clock tomorrow morning, Madam!"

Alka and I decided that we would also invite Abhineet and Gagan to the party. At the same time, we were a little skeptical, as we were not sure of his parents' reactions. But I was determined to go through with this. My training in Infy made me a stronger person; it made me realize my own loopholes and flaws. I was working on myself as I turned into someone who could be described as a very silent girl in tears most of the time.

I went to Archie's and ordered a large birthday card for him. As always, it took me an hour to select the perfect card for the perfect man. Next, we ordered the best Chinese snacks for the next day and came back to our respective homes. Alka called up Gagan and Abhineet and invited them for the party at Rahul's home the next day.

Later in the night, I called up Mama. She was very happy to hear my voice. Many times I just couldn't gather the guts to speak to her, as I didn't know what to say. I didn't want to break down in front of her, as I knew she was more hurt than I ever could be. This is a part of the process coping up with tragedies; we learn to see who is more affected by the loss. This gives all of us a chance to secretly feel good that we are better off in some ways. I told her that I was back in Ludhiana for a week and would visit her the next morning. Then it occurred to me suddenly that it was the second Wednesday of the month, and Mama's kitty party was scheduled.

Before she could answer, I said, "Oh Mama! I think you have your kitty tomorrow, so we can come up in the evening."

I heard a sigh followed by her statement, "I don't go to any kitty parties now. I have given up on my social life. I just don't feel like meeting people anymore. But, my child! You are more than welcome in this house, as I know what you meant to him. Moreover, I have to give you something that belongs to you."

"What is it Mama?" I asked.

"You come tomorrow and have a look at it yourself. It is all yours."

"Okay, Mama! As you say!" I hung up and got lost in my thoughts about what could it be. Was there something that Rahul intended to give me? No it couldn't be. He was a failure when it came to hiding surprises he planned for me. I always managed to know well in advance what was in store for me. *What could it be?* I wondered.

My phone buzzed, and I saw it was Dr. Gagan calling. I remembered the fateful night when she broke *the news* and realized it was the next morning—his birthday.

"Happy birthday to our friend, Yashi!!" she said when I answered the phone.

I just didn't know what to say but managed to thank her for her wishes. She said that she was all geared up for the special day. I knew in my heart of hearts that it was going to be a very hard day for me. Each day was, but this one had a date and numerous events attached to it. Our past influences a lot of things in our present and actions in the future.

I turned on my other cell phone; it didn't have any service, but it was still safe in my handbag. It had his picture in it. I kissed his picture and once again found him smiling through his lovely eyes.

"Happy Birthday, Baby! You are the best," I told him. I continued looking at the picture for another ten minutes and then got up from my bed and ran to the bathroom. It was his big day—rather, our big day.

Part 16

$\mathscr{I}$t was a beautiful, sunny, winter morning. I rubbed my hands after I finally got ready for the big boy's birthday. Alka was already outside my house and calling me repeatedly so that I hurried up. She had the presents I'd bought for Rahul the previous day, and we had to pick up the cake and snacks on our way to his house. I waved good-bye to my mom and told her that I would be meeting my old friends for the rest of the day to hang around with them.

Alka was driving as she noticed me lost in my thoughts again. She asked me to be cheerful and told me she understood that it was difficult for me to cope. During the drive, she tried to change the topic toward my training and life at Infosys. We reached the cake shop as I was sharing my experiences, and within minutes, a delicious-looking cake with "Happy Birthday, Rahul" written on it was in front of us. It sunk in that Rahul wouldn't cut it this time. It had to be someone else. All of a sudden, it seemed stupid to me that we were celebrating the birthday of a dead man.

Hell! No, he is right here. Just feel him, my heart scolded me and encouraged me to go ahead with the experience.

The shop owner asked, "Madam, How many candles do you need for the cake?" I was speechless. Alka realized that it was a wrong question

64

thrown right in my face. She asked for a pack of birthday candles; we paid for the stuff, proceeded toward the Chinese snack shop, and grabbed the order.

Gagan and Abhineet called to let us know that they were already waiting for us near Rahul's house. All of us decided to go in together, as it was the time we all needed strength. I was the one who rang the bell. The ding-dong memories flashed, and a tear rolled down my cheek unintentionally. Gagan asked me to control myself, as it would become very difficult to face Mama that way. I breathed hard and wiped my face; I was ready to face the world on the other side of the gate.

Mama opened the gate and welcomed us all. It seemed as if she had been waiting for us. She hugged me hard, and that hard hug was so full of inexplicable feelings. We went inside, and the view I dreaded the most was staring me straight in my eyes. It was his poster behind a fresh garland and a *tilak* on the forehead. He looked grand and intellectual in his rimless glasses. I became engrossed in watching his facial expressions and the mystery added because of his key feature—his eyes. Mama asked us to sit down, and my gang was silent. No one knew what to say.

Abhineet finally broke the silence and said, "Guys! We are here to celebrate; set the mood right." He was always an authoritative guy. I wondered how Alka kept up with him. Rahul was always understanding and flexible.

Mama got a tray full of Pepsi, and all of us helped in setting up the table for the birthday boy. The cake and the yummy snacks were all set. Then came the time for the candles. Mama judged that none of us was sure what to do.

She picked out two candles and smilingly said, "One for his past life and one for the present." She made things look so easy that I kept wondering about the strength of that woman. The candles were lit up, and the knife was lying on the table near the cake. Gagan had decorated it with a funny pink ribbon. Mama picked up the knife and handed it to me. Mama and I cut the cake together, and the rest of the clan was singing the birthday jingle. They were good doctors but pathetic singers.

I tossed away the thoughts, and Mama asked me to blow off one of the candles. I did as instructed, but a drop of tear fell on my hand. Strangely, it wasn't mine. It was Mama's. This was the situation we all dreaded. Mama excused herself after having her share of cake and went to Rahul's room, still in tears. We didn't know what to do. We all had our share and were wondering what to do next. Mama called me inside. I was about to move, as Alka looked in my eyes and asked me to be strong. I realized how amazingly good she was with her eye language and felt proud that I could understand the same with equal ease.

Mama was sitting near Rahul's study table. She had finally changed the bed sheets and cleared the mess of his books from his bed. I sat near her on the edge of his bed. Mama was holding a blue diary in her hands. She was weeping, but I said nothing, as I knew no amount of sympathies would work on her.

She looked up with tearful eyes and said, "Beta ji! This is for you. I found it when I was cleaning his wardrobe. It belongs to you. I never knew he wrote a diary."

I was shell-shocked to hold it. It was something he had written just for me. I opened the first page. It said: "For my Lips. A surprise." I wanted to have the soul of the small robot kid of the television show *Small Wonder* and read the entire diary in a flicker of a second. But I was just a human. I shakily opened the next page, and it described in detail our first meeting in Mount Abu. I was mesmerized by the artist in him. Maybe it was just the innocence of the first love. Mama handed me over two other diaries (a green one and a black one). After all, so many years could not be clubbed in one tiny booklet.

When I was about to close the first one, I scanned the last page of the blue diary. It held the words carved in his handwriting, "I want to gift this diary to Lips when we get married. My first night present to the lady I yearn to be with, this life and forever." I could not hold my tears any longer and cried out loud. Mama held me, and I noticed all the other friends entering the room. They could not comprehend why both of us were sobbing. Alka rushed to me, while Abhineet took care of Mama, and all of them tried to calm us down. I was blessed with strongest of the people around me, I must say.

I got the most well deserved gift on his big day. He changed my life, once again. I looked at his photograph in his room, where he was dressed in his lab coat and stethoscope and was giving doctor-like expressions and smiled. I thanked him in my heart as he had given me a gift that I would cherish for the rest of my life and hold close to my heart. I had each day of our relationship from his point of view. I never thought he could hide this surprise from me for so long. I fell in love with him once again.

Part 17

*W*ith the memories of his love and the taste of the cake mixed with Gems and tears, it was time for us to go back home. We bade good-bye to Mama, and Alka dropped me off at home. The weight of my handbag had increased because of the emotions in the three diaries. I rushed to my room, as it was already late evening by then. I stared at the covers of those booklets, which would give me a new reason and motive to live. At least I would not be counting days for a little while now. I gathered the guts to open the first page and reread the first meeting's description.

A prose said: "She is probably the prettiest female I have ever encountered. She has an immense charm, which drives me crazy. I shook hands with her today, and I just love the fragrance of her perfume. She is pretty good with her choice of perfumes. All the guys come to know when she is approaching the class, as she smells good from miles away. I think I like this girl. I don't know if she would agree to my offer of friendship. If she does, I would be so lucky to have a girlfriend at such an early age."

The first thought that came to my mind after reading the first meeting from his eyes was that I was a crush for him, a forbidden fruit that he wanted to taste. Strangely, I did not feel bad about it. We were kids then, and it was natural for him to feel that way. It was over time that our relationship evolved and grew. With these thoughts, I went to sleep.

The next day posed a difficult challenge in front of me. The daughter of my dad's friend and her family were supposed to visit us that afternoon over lunch. I hated socializing with strangers then and told mum that I might go out with friends, because I didn't want to be a part of the lunch. Mum objected, and it was after a heated argument that she blurted out, "They are coming to see you for their son. He is an NRI, and the family is also very good. They are jewelers in Jalandhar. We invited them so that you can spend some time with them."

My world shook once again. I never thought my folks would do something like this without my consent. According to them, I was in my mid-twenties, and that was the perfect marriageable age for a girl in India. My mom cited an example of a cousin of mine who was very choosy with guys and hence was left unmarried till the age of thirty. I rushed to Monu Bhaiya for help, but to my despair, he said that matters were beyond his control. In his opinion, I should give myself another chance in life. My next resort was Bhabhi.

She said, "Yashi! I like the family, and I think you should move on in life now. How long would you cry for the lost love?"

I felt that my family was trying to fetch a new pet for me when the old one was dead. It was a horrible experience. My mother and Bhabhi were discussing what I was supposed to wear the next day.

It was finally the next afternoon I dreaded. The family of the boy arrived in a big, posh car.

Part 18

$\mathcal{I}$ was instructed by my folks to stay inside my room until I was called. I was forced to dress up in a traditional suit, which I hated to wear. My Bhabhi even applied a little lipstick and a light makeup. Makeup was one thing I detested and never enjoyed. I thought I was faking the whole thing. I really did not understand why I was doing all this. I felt like running away from my own people; it was too much for me.

I was sitting on my bed trying to hold back my tears when I heard my mom calling me outside. "Yashi beta! Please come out."

I reluctantly went to the drawing room where everyone was sitting. Apart from my family, there was an overgrown man and a very hip-looking lady in a gorgeous suit. Then there was a good-looking young man. I found him attractive at the first sight.

Then was the formal round of introduction. Infosys had taught me how to hide the real emotions and be presentable most of the time. The overgrown man was Raj's dad, the hip-looking lady was his mom, and the attractive young man was Raj's younger brother, Rohan. Raj could not come, as he had to visit the passport office regarding some updates in his passport.

The lady asked me about my hobbies, and I answered her very confidently. I realized that I began to enjoy this different kind of interview. Then Raj's family acknowledged my achievements in terms of my placement and academic qualifications. They made it clear that although theirs was a business-class family, their elder son Raj wanted a working wife. He was a self-made man who headed the human resources department at M&S's London office. I was clearly impressed with his achievements, as I had a natural respect for intelligent people, especially people who were born with a silver spoon and still carved a niche of their own by working hard.

Then they asked me if I would be ready to relocate to the UK with Raj. I had no answer, as I never thought about a life without Rahul. It occurred to me that I had to now that he was gone forever. It was nobody's fault, but I was suffering each day without him. I told them that I needed to think on this.

His mother said, "You may meet Raj and speak to him personally regarding this issue and any other issue that you have." I took it as a crap idea, and somehow the ordeal paused for a while as they left.

My mom and Bhabhi went to our family astrologer soon after the Khannas went after lunch. The gun milan was nothing less than perfect—32.5 out of 36. The traditional Indian families have this ritual of matching the horoscopes. If the priest agrees, only then the couple is allowed to marry. Everything was hunky-dory and rosy for my parents. They wanted me to meet Raj and gave me all the positive signs that they had absolutely no problem with me marrying him.

I was very confused with whatever was happening to me. I thought I would never be able to forget Rahul. How could I get married to someone else? How could I get married at all? I felt like an unmarried widow. I called up Alka. She knew it was a little too soon for me to make such a decision. I told her that my parents were not listening to me. Alka suggested that I meet Mama and talk to her about this. I agreed, and my next call was to Mama. She called me to her place the next morning. With these loaded thoughts, I tried to sleep but could not. There were phases when I cried, when I was silent, and when I was thinking. Sometimes, every emotion got mixed up together, and the output was beyond understanding.

I went to meet Mama the next morning. I narrated the entire situation to her. I was weeping by her side. I often wondered when the stock of my tears would end.

Mama asked, "Do you think I would be able to forget him, Beta ji?"

I thought the question having an obvious answer: no. I chose to exercise my right of being silent and looked at her with questioning eyes. She further said, "I remember giving birth to him. I remember holding him in my arms for the first time. I remember his father in glad tears when he first saw him. His dad said, 'I don't believe I am holding our most beautiful and precious creation.' I remember feeding him for the first time and him waking me up in the middle of night. I did my best as a mother to soothe him in every possible way. Then I remember catching a uterine infection soon after his birth, and the doctor telling us that it could be fatal for me if I tried for another baby. It was then that his dad decided that since we had Rahul, we did not need anyone else to complete us."

"I was upset for a few days but forgot my incapability as Rahul grew up. He had my eyes, and people used to praise his eyes the most. I used to wade off the evil eyes by red chilies each time (Another Indian tradition where we try to get rid of the negative forces and energies in the universe). I remember him taking his first step, his running for the first time, his first school day. He got in one of the best schools in the city. He was such an intelligent boy. We were so proud of having him as a part of us. Then, one fine day, I got to know about your presence in his life. I was a little angry but understood that he must be very lonely in his life, so I did not say anything to him. I somehow trusted his judgment as well. I trusted my trust for his choice as soon as I met you. I accepted you as a member of this family as the time passed. I considered myself to be lucky to have a son and a daughter."

"Beta ji, I clearly remember the day when your brother and Bhabhi agreed for your alliance with him. I thought I had a perfect life. We tried to give Rahul the best life we could. But in the end, tragedy struck, and we failed. We failed to keep him alive. We failed to keep him for us and for you. You were never considered outside the family, and out of twenty-three years he lived, he was with you for eleven years. It is a big deal. But, Darling! Do you think me and hid dad have an option? We are alive and have moved on a little. His memories are sufficient for us. He hated to see any of us sad, especially you."

Mama was sad and halted her speech. I had nothing to offer her except my silence. My grief seemed trivial in front of hers. She convinced me to move on; rather, she forced me to agree for the alliance I had received.

She said, "Rahul would want to see you happy, now and forever. Promise me, you will be fair to Raj and won't take Rahul and his thoughts in your new home. This would be the right thing to do."

She made me swear on Mahtaab's picture that I would move on. With a very heavy heart and red eyes, I came back to my home and asked my parents to fix up my meeting with Raj.

Part 19

It was not an easy decision for me at all. Mama's words were harping in my head like a thunderbolt. Whatever she said was true to the core. Moving on is another name of life. But how could I move on so soon (It had not even been an year since he departed)? Now that I had agreed to meet Raj, things would be even tougher for me. I heard someone entering my room. It was my mom. She told me that I would me meeting up Raj the next day as he would be visiting us and then he would take me out for lunch. I was speechless. It was a little consoling to see my mother so happy. Only three more days were left before I was scheduled to leave for Hyderabad.

The next morning, my Bhabhi came to my room to wake me up. She is very sweet and always woke me up with wonderfully made tea and an ear-to-ear smile. That morning, it was a little different.

I was in my quilt and having my tea when my Bhabhi said, "Beta! It is time that you open up new doors for yourself. I understand it is difficult, but you can do it. Our Yashi is a fighter, and I know that. Go meet Raj; we like his profile and loved his family. Give him a chance to make you happy."

I knew whatever she was saying was correct and right, but the problem was that the heart doesn't see through brain. It has its own eyes, which just know how to love and nothing about rights and wrongs. With these thoughts, I finished my tea and got up. It was time for me to have a bath, as Raj would arrive any time. I am a late riser, so it was already eleven thirty in the morning.

I went straight in my hot water shower. With the steam coming out of the hot water and tears out of my eyes, I got ready. I went straight to the *mandir (altar)* in my home and sat next to my best friend, my Mataji, to look for answers. I had found solace in the words of Durga Chalisa every time I looked for it. I was meditating and what I saw next was simply unbelievable. I saw those green eyes telling me not to get stuck up. Those eyes told me that Yashi was a very strong person, and she could face this very easily and come out victorious. My belief in Mataji strengthened even more, and I decided to go for it with a free mind.

I heard my doorbell ringing. It was Raj. I was still in the mandir, and my mom asked me to come to the drawing room in five minutes. I was asked to serve him a cold drink and other eatables, which were right on the center table of my drawing room. I did as instructed, but at the same time, I wondered if he would ever do the same for me when I went to his home. I watched him closely as I sat opposite to him on the sofa.

He resembled his overgrown father. He had a great voice. I noticed that he was a little obese. He was very tall, six feet maybe. I am a petite, slender female. I was not sure if I would look good with him, but I am not one of those for whom looks are a priority. I wanted to know him and his achievements. We talked for a while at home, and then he asked my dad if he could take me out for lunch. My dad gladly agreed. I thought that fathers were so different when the guy is of their choice. I imagined that he would never have behaved so coolly if it was the guy of my choice.

We were in his car, and I noticed he was not one of those chivalrous guys who would open the car's door for the lady. Even though I did not want to, Raj was being compared to Rahul in my thoughts. I tried to shoo away that feeling, as I wanted to be fair to him. Moreover, the ILI sessions had taken their toll on me. Suspended judgment was what I needed at that time. Raj asked me my choice of the restaurant. As I wanted to be fair to him, I asked him to go to HMR; it was the only place where Rahul and I hadn't gone together. We went there, and surprisingly, he showed his chivalry skills there by pulling out the chair for me. I had a smile on my lips. He began asking me about my hobbies and told me about his. I felt comfortable with him and truly felt that he was my chance to move on in life. He was an interesting guy, and his obesity was not bothering me anymore.

He complemented me on my dressing sense, and I took this opportunity to tell him that I hated to wear Indian traditional suits. He said he was okay with it, as we had to live in the UK after marriage. He told me that his family really liked me and wanted to know my views on the proposed alliance. It was late evening by then, and I said, "I think it might take me a while to answer this."

With this conversation, he drove me back to my place, and my folks called him in. What I saw next was nothing less than a disaster. I saw his entire family sitting in our drawing room. Everyone was chatting, laughing, and having a nice time. We joined them.

His mother asked me, "Do you like him?"

It was a question to which any girl with basic sense of politeness would answer in affirmative. That is what I did.

I said, "He is good, Aunty ji"

Everyone smiled, and his mother held my hand and put a *kangan (bangle)* in it. I was shocked, and before I could react, my matrimonial alliance was fixed up. Yashi was formally engaged to Raj.

Part 20

$\mathscr{I}$ was shell-shocked and could not react at all. My family members were congratulating Raj's family, and next I saw my dad coming up with a gold chain and putting it on Raj's neck. Then everyone was exchanging sweets. I was forced a few barfees (a kind of sweet in India). Both of us were made to sit side by side on a sofa. The photo session began. Rohan and Monu Bhaiya started snapping pictures of us. It was all so sudden that I did not know what to do about it, whether or not I wanted to stop it.

But as of then, Raj was the man who would be my future husband. I never thought that I would be the victim of the arranged marriage system like my siblings had been. After much hullaballoo, the Khannas left. Raj did not forget to exchange phone numbers and told me that he would call me later that night. I smiled even though I did not want to. My mom hugged me like never before after they left.

Dad said, "Yashi! I am very proud of you. I knew you would never let us down."

In this country, marriage is such a big deal. In addition, there is the concept of love marriage and arranged marriage. Love marriage is always for the bad children, and arranged marriage is for people falling in any of the three categories: nerds who are too busy to fall in love, orthodox people who think falling in love is bad, or losers who lose their love or who lose in love.

Unfortunately, the third category is the saddest one, and I was a part of it. Ritu Didi was called up, and the good news was shared. She was elated, as I would be joining her in the United Kingdom soon after marriage. It was about eleven thirty that night when I went to my room. I opened Rahul's diary, as I wanted to feel his presence again. I decided to open a random page and began to read:

> She is my princess, my darling, and the love of my life, but there are times that she fails to understand me. Just like it happened tonight. I went all the way to Delhi to celebrate her birthday. I know how excited she becomes on her birthdays. She is a baby at heart, a child, who loves to open the presents with an undying enthusiasm. It was her big day, and I went to CP to surprise her. I wore my navy blue suit, as I know it is her favorite color. I think she was happy to see me, but then I said something that ruined her day. I don't understand why women are so insecure about their guys. We are getting married in a while. I mean, I might be a gynecologist one day. How will Yashi deal with that then? I must talk to her and make her understand that my eyes are just for her; I am just for her. My life and every breath I take are just for her.

> "She said something that hurt me a lot. "Rahul you are dead for me!" In the phone call tonight, she was a little pacified. I have to travel tomorrow to Ludhiana and prepare for the exam. I know she didn't mean it. I wonder what she would do if something happened to me. She cannot even tolerate a bruise on me, and she was talking about her dead Mahtaab. Anger is such a powerful emotion, especially with her. With

all my heart and soul, I love her and would show the world
by clearing the exam hurdle or, I must say, stepping stone."

The next two days just passed by with the discussions and preparations of my marriage. I took my flight from Delhi to Hyderabad, as I had to report there to human resources the next day. As my flight landed, I got a call. It was Raj.

Part 21

$\mathcal{H}$e had an amazing telephonic voice. "Hello, Yashi! I hope you have reached your destination okay. I am sorry I couldn't call that night, as I got really caught up with things. Ma was really excited about my alliance being fixed up. We went to Mata Chintapurni shrine. Then Ma took me shopping. As it is my flight next week, I want to know when you would want to get married. I would be coming back in another six months. Let's see if we can make it then. By the way, Yashi, when, at the earliest, can you come to England?"

I was not prepared for this question and answered, "Raj! Please let me get out of the airport first. Don't mind I am travelling alone and need to collect my luggage and grab a taxi for myself. I will reach ECC and call you as soon as I can."

He said, "Your wish. Call me when you are free. We need to discuss this."

I sensed arrogance and annoyance in his voice, and I certainly didn't like it. I thought that he should have understood my constraints. Then automatically, I shooed away the feelings, thinking that I didn't know him that well yet and should not be judgmental.

I collected my luggage and grabbed a prepaid taxi, as they were safer than the postpaid ones. Hyderabad was a very hot city. It was almost

February and very chilly in Delhi and Ludhiana, but it was completely different in Hyderabad. I had to remove my overcoat to be comfortable. The journey from the Begumpet airport to the Infy campus was a long and boring one. There was not much of a language problem as there was in Bangalore and Mysore. People were very fluent in Hindi and English.

I reached the campus in forty-five minutes. As any other DC, Hyderabad Development Center was equally mesmerizing. What was more mesmerizing was that it was opposite ISB (Indian School of Business), a dream B-School for many (not mine, though). I reached ECC, and it was a long and tough walk as they did not have golf carts like Mysore DC. I had to carry my eternally heavy luggage, and then, as per my company policies, I had to get it checked twice or thrice before I could check-in. Finally, I reached my room with some help from our sweet housekeeping staff. It was a huge room with two double beds. I did not understand the purpose of the same and did not bother to use my brain for that.

There was nobody else who shared the room with me, as most of the people had already reported to human resources by then. I was back from my leave. I was dead tired and went in for a bath when I heard my phone ringing. It was my mom. I realized that I hadn't called them after reaching Hyderabad, and they must be worried. I answered the phone.

"Hello, Yashi! Have you reached safely?" my mom asked.

I said, "Yes, Mom. I am perfectly fine. Just checked in the hostel. It is a brilliant room. By the way, Mom, I am in the middle of my shower. I will call you later." I did not even finish my sentence before I had another call. It was Raj again.

I hung up my mom's call and answered Raj's call. "Hi! Haven't you reached your hostel yet? I asked you to call me. Why didn't you?"

That amazing telephonic voice had extreme hints of rudeness in it, but I chose not to argue and apologized. I was too tired for that. I told him that I was in the middle of my shower. What he said next surprised me to the core, "So! You mean you cannot talk to me, but your phone was on waiting. Whom were you talking to, may I know?" Nobody had ever asked me such a question. I was shocked and felt I would be judged by my answer.

Part 22

$\mathcal{I}$ was amazed at how a person who entered my life just three days back could make me upset. Then I realized that it was not the number of days he had been a part of my life but the position he held. He was my would-be husband, and he had the right to ask. I believed that there could have been better ways for him to go about it. Very confused, hurt, and surprised, I answered him, "Raj! I was talking to my mother. She just wanted to know if I had reached safely or not."

He said, "Yes, Yashi! That is precisely what I wanted to know, but you have been too busy to even answer my questions all day long. Anyway, I do not want to ruin your mood by getting into arguments. Just relax and call me if you wish to talk." He hung up.

First, my mood was ruined to the core. Second, I was not willing to talk to him ever again. I finished my shower and, with frustration, got dressed up and called my mother. I told her the entire thing. She listened to me patiently and said, "You must take care of him. Call him more frequently if he wants. After all, he is going to be your husband. And, yes! Mrs. Khanna called, and they want the wedding to happen in December. You have about ten months for your job. Then plan to resign or take a transfer to the UK."

I tried to explain my point of view to my mother but failed, as she was not ready to listen to me. Things are so different in arranged marriages. You don't know the person, and in just one day, you are forced to love him and his family like yours own. I felt this entire system to be very stupid but had no option by that time.

I called up Raj after my mom's call. "Hello! Ms Busybee. How are you doing?" he asked.

I answered, "I am okay, just a little tired. I believe that there is something urgent that you wanted to discuss."

He said, "Yes! I wanted to tell you the great news that our guruji just called up, and he has fixed up our wedding date as December 7, 2008. Congrats, my dear would-be wife." Then he said a few more sentenced to which I just hmmed and ahhed. I had absolutely no words. It sunk in deep down that I was getting married to this man whom I did not even know properly. Then I thought that a million other girls in this country would be doing the same thing by the time my wedding date arrived. I stopped thinking, as I had thought too much that day. After the call, I went to report to my HR.

Sachin greeted me very warmly. He wasmy department's Hyderabad DC's Business Partner-HR. I found him to be a very pleasant personality. He told me that Hyderabad's base location was not certain for us and as subject to change, as was being in IVS; we would have to undergo IVS-specific training in Bhubaneshwar (another office Infy had). I did not know whether to be happy about it or sad, as I wasn't sure of my future in the company. I was not sure about my career anymore. I didn't know why my parents always forced me to achieve something in life if I had to leave it one day to join someone called a *husband* in the UK. An alien land, an alien man, and an alien family would be enough to scare anyone off. These thoughts were absolutely too much for me. All our lives as Indian kids, we are told to stay away from strangers and one fine day, we are expected to sleep with one.

I thought I would have been better off if I would have studied humanities and not competed in this big, bad perfection-driven world. All I wanted in life was love. I probably thought that way because I was never short of money. I had all the facilities in my life and at the same time was a very focused child. I owe this to my Fauji dad who tied us all together. Despite of all the good things about my family, I was unable to figure out why I was being forced to let go of my career for marriage. I decided to have a good talk about this with my mom later that day.

It was late evening by then; I went to the food court, which was really grand. Hyd DC was huge but tiny compared to Mysore and Bangalore. I finished my dinner, searched for a perfect spot in the cricket ground, and dialed my mom. It was my dad who picked up. I greeted him, and he congratulated me for my wedding date being fixed up. He sounded as if he was in the middle of something and my phone call had distracted him. He handed over the phone to my mother. She sounded worried for the preparations of my big day and was very excited for the same. I started off the topic with much reluctance.

I said, "Mom! You have always taught me to be independent, especially in terms of finances. All my life we have been told that education is very important and so is one's career. Why have your thoughts undergone a change now? Merely within a week of my engagement, you feel my career is no longer important. You were so happy when I got this job with this great company. We celebrated to the max. Now, all this seems trivial to you because you have found someone who is capable of feeding me for the rest of my life. Why suddenly am I expected to do nothing—just sit at home, raise kids, and not be career-oriented anymore? How can you expect me to forego my twenty-three to twenty-four years of training in a week? Why being ambitious is sarcasm for me today. It is okay that I am getting married. Everyone does. What is so great about it? I am not the only one who is getting married. Raj is also a party to this alliance. Why is he not expected to leave the UK and settle down in Hyderabad? Why is he not even willing to ask me if I wish to get married in December at all, or do I need some more time?"

Part 23

My mother was definitely confused about my questions, but as parents do normally, she raised her voice, as she was unable to answer me appropriately. "You have to go ahead with this, as you are a girl. Girls have to make such sacrifices. Moreover, theirs is a loving family, and Raj cares for you a lot. You are very lucky that you have got such a family. They asked for your alliance themselves, so we believe that they must not be having very high demands for dowry. I sacrificed my career for all of you, and I am glad I did that. I had the option of staying away from your father and continuing with my job as the Head of the Department of Hindi department or resigning and joining him. I consider myself wise enough to sacrifice my career for my family. You are also expected to do the same. We emphasized education, as you never know when and how tragedy can strike you in life. We wanted you to be prepared. We also want you to join your sister in the UK. Moreover, you may find yourself another job in London. I am sure you will be able to do that. Your Bhabhi has done that too. I am sure you don't regret that."

I replied, "Mom! I am not satisfied with your answer."

"It is okay, Mom answered. "Your questions show your immaturity. You will understand what we mean in the long run. Life is not what you want all the time. Trust our decision and our parenting."

I hung up. I was obviously upset but had many other things to do, like looking out for a house. I went to my hostel room and counted the number of days for my wedding. It was February, 2008 then and the beginning of my career. Before it could actually take off, the fuel was drained with the puncture called marriage. But like many other Indians, I trusted my parents more than my own judgment. So I gave in to the fact that I would be Mrs. Raj Khanna and wanted to feel happy about this decision of mine (rather my family's).

My next phone call was to Raj. His mother picked up. It was about 11 PM then. I wished her Namaste. She said, "In our families, daughters in law wish Pairi Pauna (equivalent to touching the feet)." Not that I did mind it but the hip lady's tone was no more hip. I apologized and asked if Raj could be reached. She said, "Raj was tired and so he has slept. I will tell him to speak to you tomorrow." What more could I say? I hung up. Thinking about all that happened in the last few months, I slept.

It was 9 AM that I heard the bell of my hostel room ring. I opened the door. It was the housekeeping lady. She had come to clean up the room. I was late for office and went straight inside the bathroom to get ready. The housekeeper was doing her job but was cheerful enough and asked me why I hadn't finished the tea. She wanted to refill the sachets. I told her that I was not much of a tea person and liked coffee better.

With this discussion, I was concurrently getting ready. I was amazed at how they made up the worst untidy room of Infy tidied up in say twenty minutes. I went to Sachin to Building number 19 and got myself a cubicle allocated. It had been long that I had logged on to Sparsh (Internal Infosys Intranet). I raised AHDs for asset allocation. I was about to leave for lunch that Raj called up. "Hi Baby! How are you doing?" I did not have the guts to tell him that I was leaving for lunch. I had never felt so intimidated in my entire life. I tried to sound cheerful

89

and answered him, "I am going for lunch but it is OK, we can talk." He threw some sarcasm about me being very busy and not sparing enough time for him. Then I tried to change the topic and inquired about his job profile. He sounded reluctant to discuss that and started flirting with me. I was very tired and hungry to death and that Raj flirting with me was the last thing I wanted then. But my mom's words, "Keep Raj and his family happy, if you love us" harped in my brain. Moreover, I thought that talking to him will make our relationship evolve. Not that I had any option to run away from the situation. Then in the middle of his flirting session, Raj asked me something to which I lied. He asked me, "Have you ever been in love before loving me?" The second half of the question was an overstatement (I was not in love with Raj) and I did not know what to say about the first half.

Part 24

"Raj! What kind of question is this?," I said. "No babes! I need to know each and every thing about you. Your past, present and your future." I was tempted to fall in that trap but trusted my gut feeling to test this relationship a little more. I said, "No Raj! I have never been involved in something like this. Have you been?" He said, "Though I live in London and was in an all-boys boarding. I have always believed in arranged marriage as I feel that my mother knows what or who is best for me. I love my mom to bits. She is very excited about my marriage. I must tell you that you are very fortunate that you have a mom-in-law like my mom. She is the best in the world." The hip-looking lady had definitely made her mark on her son. It was a very different way of praise I had heard about a mom from a son.

I noticed that he could talk a lot and even ignore the other person's statements while talking. It was a little irritating for me but I ignored for reasons unknown. We spoke about our marriage which was ten months later. Raj seemed pretty excited about it. He mentioned that since he belongs to a high-class family of Jalandhar, they usually have lavish weddings. I sensed it as a hint but since it could be later generalized by him, I chose not to argue. I also feel that he was successful in dominating me in less than a week. I began losing my confidence and could not express me in a way I used to. I turned into a very silent and sad girl. I joined my training batch friends in Hyderabad. It was after a week; I vacated the comfort of Infy guest house and moved to my apartment in a sad place called Tollichowki. I did not like Hyderabad's climate as it was too hot most of the times. I adjusted myself to the kind of lifestyle I was in. I observed that I was a very flexible and adaptable female. Or maybe, I had better reasons to crib in life, I ignored these trivial issues.

Raj used to call off and on. His favorite topics of discussion with me included his mother's praises, his family and gossips about his aunts. I was amazed at how an HR manager could waste his precious time discussing about his tayiji (hindi word for older aunt) and chachiji (hindi word for younger aunt). But he did it and did it with a lot of ease. I was never a gossip person as these things were never encouraged in my family. The academic background of my family could have been a reason behind this. His family was not at all educated. He was the only one who finished a Masters in their family history. He was regarded with great respect and love in his circle. His self made attitude was the only reason I agreed to meet him. Though they were filthy rich, I saw how education can make a difference in one's personality.

I was allocated to an internal project in Hyderabad. We had our IVS specific training wound up in Hyderabad itself. It saved me the pain to travel to BBSR. I was contended at last. My project was going on well. Raj had left for UK. He used to call me once or twice a week. According to me, it was a little less frequent for a couple to talk this less. I decided to make a move on my part and decided to talk to him at least once a day. It went well for the initial weeks. He was happy gossiping about all the people who had wronged his family and his oh-so-innocent mother. I sensed that whenever I try to talk about his job or our future, either his phone's battery went off or he was reminded of something very urgent which was nowhere in picture when he was gossiping about what a bitch his Chachi (aunt) had been. I could sense something very fishy going on but could not put it in words. Once, I was unable to

92

reach him for an entire weekend. I was really mad at him. I spoke to his mother. She said that he must be working as he had a hectic weekend which he mentioned to her. I felt that there were a lot of critical things which were mentioned to Mummyji and not me. I tried to get rid of the feeling by calling it useless jealousy. Maybe, I was indeed getting attached to that man.

My friends thought that it was a very natural thing to happen and advised me to relish the fact that I had moved on. I used to feel guilty about not missing Rahul that much then but more bothered about how Raj would be and what he would be doing. Three months down the line sitting at my desk, I felt a spark. I was expecting his call when I got an unexpected call. It was some number from Pune. "Hello! Is it Yashi!."

"Yes it is, Who is this?"

"Hi! This is PKS from Pune office. We have a billable project requirement for you in Pune. You are required to travel to Pune over this weekend and join Phase I office coming Monday. Sachin would take care of all the formalities. Please raise travel request for your travel and plan accordingly."

"Oh OK! It is too soon, isn't it?"

"Ya, that's the way things go on when we have critical business requirements,. Hope you do not have a problem with the offer?"

"Absolutely not! I am a flexible employee. I am ready to relocate. Thank you."

He hung up.

Part 25

$\mathcal{T}$he journey to Pune was hectic but comfortable. I had my cab waiting right outside the airport. It felt so good to travel to the city which had a rocking night life and was full of lively people. It took me an hour and a half to reach Infy Phase 1 campus. I felt the climate was a lot more favorable than Hyderabad's. The guard at the campus' gate directed me to Phase 2 campus as ECC was not in Phase 1. This meant shedding off another hundred rupees for a five minutes trip. It was an expensive city, no doubt. I checked in the hostel. It was the third DC in six-seven months of my joining with Infy. I thought I was about to create a record of being posted to every DC of this company in the shortest time span.

I relaxed for the rest of the day. I had to report to PKS the next morning. I had my project's induction scheduled for the entire day. It went on very well. I liked the application and thought I would nab the maximum number of bugs. Down the line, it proved to be a great learning experience, professionally. I was learning to balance my profession with Raj's and family's calls. I was getting better at it with each passing day. Caught in the balancing act, I got an email for an upcoming project party. The venue was a posh night club in Pune. I had very few friends in Pune. I felt my personality underwent a sea-change after Rahul's demise and my engagement added fuel to the fire. I lost interest in interacting with people. All I did the entire day was work very hard and go home, cook for myself and then sleep. I had no roommates as I was putting up at Sandhya aunty's bungalow in Aundh. She was Col. Dahiwalkar's wife and a family friend. My parents had a very long association with the Dahiwalakrs. She was a Maharashtrian (A western starte in India, Mumbai is its capital) and an extremely warm lady. Her son, Sameer bhaiya was also an army officer then. I had a comfortable life there.

I thought that the upcoming party would help me open up to new people and make a few friends. I was getting better at work but was losing out on my confidence in interacting with people. Raj's dominating nature was also a key factor in this. I got dressed up with all my heart for the first time after I came to Pune. I wore a little make-up and silver danglers. I appreciated myself in the mirror after a long time. I heard my phone ringing. It was Sunny, my colleague who was outside my house. He was supposed to pick me up and drop me later that night as I had no conveyance of my own there. I locked the main gate and saw him staring at me with amazement in his eyes. I smiled and asked him, "What is wrong?" He said, "I wish everyday was a project party. You are looking gorgeous." I thanked him for the compliment and we drove till the club. My entire team was present and since I was the latest entry in the gang, I was told to introduce myself. After the introduction, I sat next to Niki and Anne, my team mates. I saw people in my team were drinking and smoking. I had a great repulsion for people who used to overindulge themselves, just because something was being paid for by the company. Unfortunately, there were too many of them.

I tried not to bother myself much. DJ was loud and my colleagues were high and dancing. I was silently enjoying my Pepsi. Suddenly, I felt a tap on my shoulder. It was Sunny asking me to dance with him. I refused as I did not enjoy dancing very much. He was disappointed but did not force me much. He later got me a glass of Pepsi, which tasted funny. I had a few sips but could not finish it. I sensed something fishy. I asked

Anne to try my drink and check it. She was sure it had Vodka mixed in it. I was really disappointed in Sunny. More than disappointment, it was a sense of anger prevailing over me. I confronted Sunny there itself. I asked him, "I think you gave me your drink." He said, "Hell! No. Not possible. I got this especially for you." I argued, "Sunny, this has alcohol in it. You know very well that I do not drink. I must remind you that crossing your line with me would invite trouble for you. I am not a girl who would take this crap from you or anyone, as a matter of fact." He apologized and said, "Yashi! I just wanted to play a little prank on you." I was annoyed to the max and saw PKS coming towards us. He was our PM and gathered from Anne and Niki whatever happened. He warned Sunny and told me not to ruin my mood over something like this. He assured me that this would be taken care in a formal manner the next day in office. I accepted Sunny's apology and finished my dinner fast. I was in no mood to talk to Sunny, let alone go along with him at night. I asked PKS to arrange a drop for me. He did that. Overall, it was a sad evening for me. I was in Varun's car and something happened which aggravated my gloom to a higher level.

Part 26

"*R* aj calling . . ." I answered the call. Varun's choice of music was hip-hop. Raj knew it was not my kind-of music. After the formal hello, he asked me, "Where are you?" I answered, "I was at a project party and I am on my way to home."

"You are with whom?"

"Raj! I am with Varun, my team mate. I would reach home in five minutes."

"So! You are busy with someone else at 1 AM and do not have time for your fiance'."

"It is not that Raj! I . . . I . . . I would call you back." I did not want to create a scene in front of Varun.

I reached home and called him, even before changing my clothes. He was very angry as why hadn't I taken his permission for the party. I answered, "My entire team was there and I don't have many friends here, so I thought if I go, it will be beneficial for me here."

"Yeah! So that you can have more night-outs there. Yashi! You know what! I feel your job is creating a lot of problems in our relationship. I want you to leave it and relax at home. Prepare for our wedding nicely. It is once in a lifetime event and make it grand. I trust you but I do not trust people around."

"Raj! I do not wish to leave my job. I have signed a bond here and I need to complete one year in this firm. I think it will help me a lot when I would look for a job in London."

"Who says, I want you to work when you come here? I want you to be at home and take care of the family. I can give you the best of the facilities. You need not work darling" His tone softened.

"But Raj . . . I have worked very hard to reach this level. It is not about the need to work, it is about the want to work." I personally felt that it was an international wastage if we don't utilize our talents and did not work, even when we could.

He yelled at me and told me to set my priorities straight in life. He even hinted me that he would not hesitate to call off the relationship. My sobs were not making any difference to that man. He hung up and I went to my room crying all the way.

I opened my wardrobe to change. I felt that something fell on my right foot. It was Rahul's diary. It exponentially increased my tears. I picked it up and cried like hell, holding the diary in my hands, went outside in the garden. I looked up to the heavens for a sign. I saw Mahtaab, smiling at me and trying to comfort me. I slept in the garden that night.

I got another phone call that morning that was about to change my life.

Part 27

It was Raj's mother and as usual, her hip-tone blended with the dominance she had genetically transferred to her son. "Namastey Ma, How are you?" She answered, "Namastey Yashi, I would be expecting a pairi pauna next time. Anyways, I had to discuss something important with you. Are you free?" (As if I had an option to argue with her!!)

"Yes Ma, Please tell me what is it?"

"Yashi, Raj called up very late at night yesterday and was very angry with you. I believe there was some party in Pune and it went on till very late. You came back in some stranger's car, someone from your company. Is it true?"

"Yes Ma, it was my project party and I came back with Varun, my team mate, not exactly a stranger."

"Yashi! We are a very respectable family of Jalandhar and you are our daughter-in-law. Your father-in-law is very worried and upset about what happened last night. You know, it can get repeated and none of us want that. We want you to leave your job and come to Punjab ASAP. As far as pacifying Raj goes, that I will do. I hope I have made myself very clear."

"But Ma, I have signed a bond here and I cannot break it. It has legal implications. Moreover, this would mean me letting go this career totally." I think the disappointment in my voice reached the other end.

"I was expecting an answer like this. Raj and his dad will no way understand you. I can convince them, if you come to Chandigarh at least."

"But Ma, I still have one more month to have this project wrapped up. I will only be free by beginning of October. My bond is till November BTW."

"OK, I want you to get a transfer to Chandigarh. At least, you will be near us and within reach. Do that as it is very important for all of us. And yes, please call Raj by afternoon and apologize. He was very upset. You know, he is all alone there in UK and he cares for you a lot."

She hung up. I was shell shocked after the conversation. I knew it was unfair but decided to talk to PKS about this and see if something could be done. I got ready quickly and caught the 9AM bus to office. As soon as I reached the ODC, I sent out a meeting request to PKS. He accepted it. I went to his cubicle five minutes before the meeting time owing to my anxiety.

"Yes Yashi! How are you this morning? I have called Sunny also. He will be here any minute."

PKS thought that I wanted to discuss the last night's incident but I had something else on my mind which bothered me more than Sunny. I was trying to find words for my current concern and Sunny entered.

"Hi PKS, So you called me!" he said embarrassed. "Sunny, I hope you are sober enough to explain the blunder you committed last night."

"Yes PKS, I am very sorry for whatever happened. I am sorry Yashi. This would never ever be repeated. Please don't escalate the issue and resolve it here itself."

"Ok! Sunny, You may leave now. Yashi, you stay."

Sunny left and I stayed, as directed. PKS continued, "Yashi! It was a genuine concern that you raised last evening. I believe you and Sunny cannot remain in the same project anymore. I want to ask you if you are ready to leave the project or you want me to move him out."

I sensed this as an opportunity to ask for a transfer to Chandigarh. He showed positive signs and told me that he would get back to me by evening. Later that evening, I got a call from PKS telling me that my transfer to Chandigarh has been approved and I am required to join CHD DC two weeks later. So there I was, planning another transfer and incrementing my DC count. I felt life straightening itself for once. I was genuinely happy as I would be able to see my parents every weekend and keep Raj and his mom happy all in one go.

Two weeks passed and I was in Chandigarh DC. North India, finally I thought I would give my "Bharat darshan (Domestic travel)" a break and was looking forward for the videsh darshan (International travel) as my wedding approached. After all, 7th Dec, 08 was not far away. Only two months to go and I would be with Raj as my lawfully wedded husband. I was getting to know him better with each day. I was not missing Rahul that much then as I was caught up in wedding shopping and arrangements. Raj used to call me every alternate day and inquired in detail about all the plans and proceedings. He seemed very excited for the wedding and luckily, his excitement touched me. I started liking that dominating guy as I now knew how to handle him. Or at least, that is what I thought.

Part 28

$\mathscr{I}$t was Karvachauth (husband's day) next week (last week of Oct). Women in India are expected to fast without even sipping a drop of water for the entire day; of course, food is not an option either. My would-be mother-in-law visited me and gave me goodies for the festival (or Sargee), one evening before the fast. I had never kept a fast like this in my entire life. At the same time, I was looking forward for it. After all, I was getting married to this guy and had all the reasons to believe that fasting can bring long life to him. I think I was scared of losing him (maybe I was getting attached to him or maybe I had lost Rahul in the past). The hip-looking lady was looking amazingly Indian when she was explaining me the norms for the upcoming day. I developed a sense of immense respect for her and the festival. She left later that evening and I was too involved in my thoughts about the next day.

I woke up at 4, the next day and with Mom and Bhabhi, I ate the morning sargee. It was such a divine feeling. Raj had carved a place for himself in my Rahul-filled heart. I was happy to move on as life says, "Move On" at every step. I thought about Raj and our upcoming marriage all day long. It was about 8:30 PM and Raj called me up.

"Hey Darling! How is the fast going?"

"I am a little hungry but very thirsty."

"Don't worry, Mr. Moon is out. I saw it on the internet. Go see for yourself."

I rushed outside and ran up the terrace, with the phone in my hand. I yelled at the top of my voice, "Ma, Bhabhi . . . Moon is there." I was so elated.

"Yashi! I want to tell you something. I also fasted for you today and look at the moon and make your fast a success."

Mom and bhabhi were there in no time, so was Dad and Bhaiya. I prayed and looked up at the moon. Mahtaab was smiling at me again. Raj was on call with me and my heart drifted towards Rahul again. I felt caught up badly. I almost had tears in my eyes. I had an indication that Mahtaab wants me to move on with Raj and he would still be by my side. I had a hearty chat with Raj after the prayers. I was about to sleep when I received another call.

It was Mama. "Hello Beta ji! How are you?"

"Hey! Mama! Namastey. I am fine, you tell."

"Beta ji! Please come for the Havan (prayers) tomorrow morning."

"What Havan Mama and why?"

"Did you forget, It will be one year tomorrow that Rahul left us. It is 24th Oct."

I was devastated at what Mama said. I had actually forgotten the date. I considered myself to be good with dates and numbers but failure slapped me hard this time. All I could say was, "Yes Mama! I will come tomorrow."

The memories of him slipping out of my hands and life struck me again and I cried myself to sleep. I woke up next morning and began to get ready for the Havan. I was usually a late riser, so my mother inquired, "Where are you going?"

"It's the barsee (Death Anniversary) of a friend. I am going to his place for the Havan."

"Yashi! You know it is your marriage in a month. It is very inauspicious to go to ominous places. You are not going anywhere and that is final."

I cried, yelled, fought but my family did not listen to me. I thought lying would have been a better option.

Part 29

$\mathscr{I}$t was devastating for me that I could not attend his barsee owing to the superstitious nature of my family. I had no option but to tell Mama the truth. She absolutely understood it. I did not have to lie to her. Though, I could sense a deep regret in her voice but she carefully hid it. She wished me best luck for my future and asked for a wedding invite for herself. I was surprised at her demand as hers was the first name in my list. I said, "Mama! How could you think that I can go on without your blessings?"

"No Beta ji! I believe that moving on involves a lot of compromises on the relationships of the past. A tree must shed its old leaves if it wants new ones." Mama's one liner said a lot of things. I pondered over the thoughts for a while and decided to accompany my mom and Bhabhi for the Bridal Lehanga's (Indian wedding dress) shopping. I started developing mixed feelings regarding buying my lehanga exactly after a year that he went. I was confused as I knew it was him who was giving me signals from up above the skies that he was happy with the marriage or he wanted me to be reminded of him in everything I was doing. Nevertheless, I missed him though I was developing a liking towards Raj and his family. I got attached to Rohan as he used to call me every alternate day and updated me about the groom's side preparations. It was big news in his family as no man had ever fasted for his wife in their entire lineage. I was secretly elated about the fact that my man wanted a long life for me. I was used to Raj and his ways which were uniquely cute. I knew I would have to work hard if I had to adjust in that family. I was ready for the same as I already made a lot of adjustments by then.

I started wearing Indian suits whenever the hip-looking lady paid a visit to us. I even began enjoying getting overly dressed up at times. I was learning to apply liner and mascara. These things were literally alien to me a few months ago. Raj expressed once that he would want me to learn how to wear nice eye make-up. I was tuned off at that point as I hated wearing any kind of make-up then. I faked a smile and agreed. With these thoughts hovering, Yashi (with a perfect eye-liner and Mascara) went for her Lehanga shopping. Nilibar Stores, Out of the displayed twenty pieces, I selected the best one. Bhabhi was happy that I was finally enjoying the idea of getting married. The lehanga made a big hole in my brother's pocket but strangely, he was glad with that. He treated me like his daughter and the entire responsibility of the celebrations was on the shoulders of my bro and bhabhi.

I joined my office the next Monday. It was the first week of November and my heart pounded as my wedding date approached. Days passed by and Miss Yashi sent out an e-invite and "sweets at my desk" mails to all those who mattered at those who did not. After all, I was supposed to be on a month's leave after that day. Last time, my signatures read Miss Yashi. I even wondered the inequality between men and women. Guys would me Mr. before and after their marriage. I hated guys for this privilege.

Last week of November was when Raj was flying back to India. He reached safely at Amritsar Airport. I was dying to meet him. I was happy that a bond was created before the D-Day. He was supposed to meet me the next day of his arrival.

I got dressed up in a nicely with gleaming eyes and an ear to ear smile, greeted my would-be husband. We had a nice romantic date and he showered me with presents. Both domestic and international. He judged my choice of perfumes and bought me some really nice ones, "Romance-Ralph Lauren," my all time favorite stole the show and so did Raj. We discussed about our future and he seemed very excited about our big day, which was just a week away. Both of us had butterflies in our tummies.

Part 30

7-Dec-2008

$\mathcal{T}$he day which was going to change me and my life forever (Though I was not short of such days in my life). Alka and Gagan were by my side. The last few days went off amazingly well with fervor, fun and frolic. Punjabi weddings are very lavish and so was mine. Punjabis are known to compromise on anything but style. It involved a series of hunky-dory functions. People came, ate, enjoyed and pin-pointed the gray areas in the arrangements. It was despite the fact that my family had worked very hard in the last few months to make the ceremonies a grand success. This was the major demand of Raj's family as well and was taken care to the best of our capabilities. In the midst of crowd comprising of my relatives (known and many unknown), my pals found some time with the bride. Then Alka said something which was much unexpected.

"Yashi, I would like you to hand over Rahul's diaries to us and move on completely. It will be unfair on your part if you carry the burden of your past in your future. Some burdens are better dealt with if they are shed off in time."

"Alka! What are you saying? I cannot do that. Those diaries are his last gift to me."

"Yashi! Alka is right. We know it would be difficult for you but trust me, it is for your betterment." Added Gagan.

They had a valid point and my artistic turned logical mind understood the idea behind that. With a very heavy heart and millions of tears in my eyes, I handed over the packet containing Rahul's cards and diaries to my friends. They promised to keep it safe. I immediately felt released, I don't know why!!

I went to the beauty parlor in the afternoon and there was a very experienced beautician lady dressing up about 20 brides. I wondered that all of us shared the same wedding date. People were dressed up nicely, or I would say, overdressed. I was a little worried as how would I look. The make-up ordeal began and lasted for about four hours (hairstyle, Chunri setup, Lehnga drape, eye make-up, base make-up and the overall . . . These are the few I can recall but I am sure, there were more.)

The experienced lady's hard work finally paid off and I was amazed with the end result. I looked my best in 24 Years. I thought I looked better than the other 19 brides present there. My cousin came to pick me up and he was not at all short of compliments for me. My aunt applied a black tika (to fight the evil eyes) at the back of my ear. I felt very special. The baraat was on time unlike most baraats in India. I was in the add-on room of the marriage palace. People were visiting me and showering their blessings on me. The photographers were very busy and wanted me to throw weird poses at the lens, which I refused to do. They were a little annoyed but so was I, with a lot of heavy accessories on myself (Choora, Kaleerey, and what not).

The wedding went off very well. Raj was looking very good that day. He was a handsome, tall man (though a little obese, but it did not matter to me anymore). I was planning to starve him until he made it to his perfect size. Then came the hardest moment for any girl post pheras, the Bidaai.

My family sent me away with a heavy and happy heart. We were at the marriage palace's gate that Mama came and hugged me and bade me a goodbye packed with lots of luck. I was on my way to the florally decorated car when my ever active tear. I was crying uncontrollably when Raj held my hand to console me. I felt a huge mix of varied emotions. In the car, which Rohan was driving and Ma was in the front seat, I felt as if I was taking up a new transfer somewhere to some DC of Infy. The difference was the pomp and show and that I was carrying on myself a hell lot of make-up and a lot of emotions.

After about an hour's journey, we reached Jalandhar, where I was greeted with lots of excitement. After the formal entry or the vadhu-pravesh, Raj took me to his room. We were really tired after the processes and procedures of the milestone called *"The Great Indian Wedding."*

In Raj's room, when we were relaxing, Raj's phone buzzed. He seemed a little uncomfortable. He went outside to take the call. I was not curious to know who it was as all I wanted to do that night was to catch up for my lost sleep and gear up for the challenges coming up the next day.

Part 31

The Next Morning (11:30AM)

I woke up when I heard people laughing outside. I don't catch up sleep at new places but I was so tired that even the novelty of the bed left me unaffected. I woke up but did not find Raj around. I sat on my bed for a few minutes as I was not sure what to do. I could still feel the traces of make-up on my face, though I washed it about a million times. My hair wanted a wash badly, thanks to the chemicals the experienced lady dipped them into. I rushed in the shower. It took me an hour to get ready, for the first time in my life. The hustle-bustle outside was increasing exponentially but none seemed to bother about me. I thought that they forgot the new addition in the family. I was almost ready when I heard a knock at my door. It was Rohan (Raj's brother), who wanted me to come out for some silly post-marriage games. He led me to the drawing room where I was greeted by the relatives of all shapes and sizes (there were so many of them). Then began the ordeal of "Pairi Pauna," which I enjoyed somehow.

The games were fun; they were more like an induction in the new family. Most of the relatives went back by evening. Some were scheduled to leave the next day. I did not find real quality time with Raj, mainly because of the presence of so many people around. The hip-looking lady and now my mom-in-law was sitting in some distant corner of the drawing room and threw real grim expressions. She was actually talking to Raj's chachi (younger aunt). "Yashi! Please come here!" I obeyed and sat next to them. She said, "What am I listening?" I said, "What Ma, What happened?"

"Yashi! Chachi's family was not taken care of properly during the ceremonies. She is complaining that your mother only paid attention to Tayiji (elder aunt) and not her. I absolutely had no answer to what she said. I had no option but to apologize. I felt extremely uncomfortable and wanted to run away to my room to weep but could not. I controlled my tears. Both the cribbing ladies stood up and went away. Raj observed something happening. He came and sat next to me. "What happened? You look upset. Everything okay?"

I did not want to create a scene so I said, "Ya Ya, all well. You tell, Mr. Busy. No time for your wife?" He said, "Let's go to our room as I wish to tell you something." He looked stern.

With millions of thoughts and zillions of emotions, I escorted him. He bolt the door. I found a place on the bed. He said, "Yashi! I am not at all happy about the feedback I am getting about the marriage. This is not done. We have not asked for anything as dowry. All we wanted was a grand wedding and good care of our guests. But what has happened is a disaster."

"Raj! What are you talking about? My family worked for last six months to make this a success. I think the wedding was awesome and pretty lavish."

"YA Yashi! That is what *you* think? Relatives are taunting us about getting a girl from the service class family. Even I think it was a mistake. My dad is so upset. You know he is a BP patient and he won't be able to survive this social insult."

"But Raj! My parents asked you about any specific demand. And they have done their best, maybe more than their best, trust me. This is not fair. Just because your relatives are not happy, you cannot go on and insult my parents this way."

"Yashi! Don't you dare talk to me like that! I hope I have made myself clear. I will not take shit from you and your family. Your brother and dad should come and apologize for the disaster last night."

He stood up, threw the cushion that was in his hand at the mirror and went out slamming the door.

I realized what a mess I was in. My world crashed, *once again*.

Part 32

All the relatives left by the next day. Talks were on for our honeymoon. Raj decided to get a package booked for Singapore and Malaysia for next week. He asked me as if my approval mattered!! I was supposed to travel to Ludhiana with Raj for the Phera (When the girl visits her parents' home first time after wedding) the same evening. On our way to Ludhiana from Jalandhar, I asked Raj not to bring up the topic he discussed with me. I said, "Raj, it will hurt my parents a lot." He said, "I don't care, their negligence has hurt my parents as well. Yashi! I am a very straightforward person and rather than keeping this to myself, I would tell them and ease myself."

I kept quiet for the rest of the journey. He was a very rude man. I was wondering what he would say. We almost reached our place when mom-in-law called up. "Yashi! Please tell Raj to stop at a florist and a sweet shop. I want you to buy a nice, expensive bouquet and some sweets. I am sure you mustn't be aware of this. This is how we greet our relatives in our families." With choking voice, I said a yes and hung up. I conveyed the message to Raj and he did as instructed. We were greeted very warmly back home. I wept hard as soon as my mom hugged me. I never missed the bunch as much in my entire life as I did in the last two days. I was praying secretly that Raj behaves properly at my place.

But Mataji chose not to answer my prayers this time and Raj showed his true colors in the first half an hour of meeting my family. He was no more the cordial guy my family saw. Out of the blue, he said, "Uncle, I wish to share some feelings with you. I hope you will take me seriously." All were silent except the twins who were still excited to see their Yashi bua in traditional clothes, a rare sight for them.

"Yes Raj! Go ahead."

"Uncle, My family is really unhappy and dissatisfied with the wedding arrangements. It was the last wedding in your family for this generation but the first one for us. My father would like to see you next week. Rest, I advise you not to take any tensions about it. We will sort this out ASAP."

I could sense gloom on my Fauji dad's wrinkled face. He was a master in hiding his emotions but he never concealed his anger, if at all it existed. "All right Raj! I would come to meet Mr. Khanna. Anything else, Beta." My father was very polite. I thought he would tell Raj to mend his ways at least but my expectations did not fulfill.

Most of my Ludhiana visit went off in tears. I tried to hide my problems from my family as I did not want to bother them. I said, "I am happy, just the initial adjustments and I'll be fine." I think they believed me.

We were supposed to fly to Malaysia the next Friday. That was when, my parents came to meet me an evening before (or to apologize the overgrown man for the so-called discrepancies in the ceremony). Everyone was sitting in the drawing room when my father-in-law came up with a glass of whiskey in his hand. He offered a drink to my dad and brother but they refused. Nobody in my family drank alcohol.

F-I-L sat comfortably next to my father and put his arm on my dad's shoulder while all of us watched. He said, "You get discount on any kind of liquor in the CSD, right?"

My dad nodded. He continued, "Still! All you offered in the wedding was Teachers. We were expecting Chivas. Anyways, that is not all. No car, no flat, no nothing. I thought you were matured enough to understand the needs of your daughter but I was wrong. A service class man would remain a service class for his entire life. Anyways, I must tell you that I am sending the kids to Singapore and Malaysia tomorrow at my expense. I love my children and Yashi is my child now. Rest, we would visit you once they are back from their trip and talk in detail."

I wondered what other detail that stupid man missed. I wanted to slap him right in the face but the values my folks inculcated in me, stopped me to do so. My father submissively apologized. I could see no reason except that he wanted to see me happy. I took my bhaiya aside and looked in his eyes inquiringly. He said, "Yashi! Don't worry. All will be well. We would satisfy their demands. You just be your best here and don't give them another chance to complain."

"But Bhaiya! We have already spent a fortune at the wedding. I don't understand what they want."

"Yashi! All I want from you is to enjoy your honeymoon. You would anyways leave India soon and go to UK, right. So don't bother and relax."

My family left later in the night after the insult session. I had never imagined my life to be like this. I still took the flight next morning (not that I wanted to go but I had no option). The honeymoon was ok. It was more like an educational tour with a hint of romance (romance: as per Raj and hormones/lust: as per me). I realized that we were very different people but the worst was yet to come. He did not hand me over even a single dollar of that currency (Malaysian Ringets / Singapore Dollars). I felt so bloody dependent on him. I was not brought up like that. I was never treated like this ever in my life, the way this man treated me in the last ten days.

He used to force me to drink but I somehow managed to keep myself away from that. He used to call me, "DownMarket, Low Standard" and names like that. But I knew I had been very disciplined in my life in terms of drinking and smoking, so I was very firm on my belief. He overindulged himself in alcohol one night and expressed that he wanted to talk to me about something. I sensed trouble but was too scared to even argue. We were in M hotel's room at the twelfth floor in Singapore.

"Yashi! I have heard that your father has a farmhouse in Ludhiana. I think you must tell him to sell it so that we can buy a nice flat in UK."

I could not control myself anymore. "Raj! This is not done. You guys never put out demands like this before the marriage. What is this now? I am educated and I would work hard to keep you and your family satisfied. Please spare my family. Please."

The drunken man threw his can of beer on the ground. The carpet was soiled badly. He rushed towards me and held my hair. I used to tie them in a ponytail, which was very painfully in his drunken hands. He smelled bad. He shouted, "What did you say? You would not do this? Do you know marrying you has ruined me thoroughly?"

I said, "Raj, you are hurting me. Please leave me. Leave me alone."

"Leave you . . . That is exactly what I always wanted but Mom never agreed."

"What are you talking about, Raj! Leave me alone please. Leave my hair."

He shouted something very abusive and next I remember myself on the ground. It took me a while to realize that I was punched. Yes! I was punched very hard, right in my nose and I was probably bleeding. My left nostril was oozing a lot of blood and this man paid no attention. He blabbered something and went off to sleep. I spent the entire night crying and covering my wound up.

But many such wounds were yet to occur. We were supposed to fly back to India the next day.

Part 33

$\mathcal{I}$t was a five and a half hour flight back to Delhi. It took us another ten hours to reach Jalandhar. The tiredness enhanced with each passing minute. My desire to live was almost dead. I was sick of my life. But I guess it was a little too soon to give up. Yashi was not the types who gave up easily. I did not talk to Raj for the entire journey, neither did he. I think he did not even realize that he was wrong. Chances were high that he did not even remember that he hit me the previous night. We reached Raj's home. The hip-looking lady made nice tea for us but served it with disgusting stares. We freshened up and it was dinner time. At the dining table, the overgrown man and the obese son hurdled abuses at me for not bringing enough dowry. I felt like killing myself there and then. The latest insult session paused when Raj received a phone call. He again went out to answer it. I left my food mid-way and went to my room, thinking about what next to do. I was supposed to join Infy back the next week and thought it would provide me some solace at last. Raj had to fly to UK, the next week as well. Things eased out a little. The frequency of quarrels reduced owing to increasing dinner invites.

I spoke about our marriage registration on the breakfast table. It was about five days, we had in hand. I was again answered in an abrupt manner (I was getting used to these mannerisms). They said, the marriage would be registered in April when Raj would come back next to take me. I innocently agreed. But it was another red flag, I missed.

I went to Chandigarh and Raj left for UK. His calls reduced exponentially. He rejected my calls as well. He was even distancing himself from Ritu didi. I used to visit Jalandhar almost every weekend. The hip-looking lady and the overgrown man left no occasion to insult me unutilized. Rohan was the only one, who was a little gentle on me. Several months passed by and I was a decent cook as this is what the MIL expected and I was an early riser now who wore contact lenses and make-up, the first thing after getting up.

I lost out on all my hobbies and refused to talk to most of my friends. I was not the same Yashi anymore. One fine morning, the overgrown man called me up. I was getting ready for office. He started shouting at me, "Yashi! We know what you do there. Just resign and pack your bags. You are not working anymore and that is an order." He did not listen to me and hung up. It was then I called up my dad and told them I would be resigning the same day. He said he was ok with it if I was.

I went to the office and sent out a meeting request to Neha Bishnoi, my unit BP-HR. I filed my e-separation and called MIL to share the news. What she said was again uncalled for. "Send me a screenshot as a proof." "Ma! This is against our policies, so I would not be doing that."

"Why are you bothered? You are not going to work for this company. Just do as I say."

"No Ma! I would not and I am sure about it." I hung up.

I received my mother's call in twenty minutes. I think she was crying. She asked me to apologize to them. I agreed to apologize but told her that I would not violate the company's policy.

Neha validated my esep and it reached the next step. I went to Jalandhar the coming weekend.

I was greeted with yet another shock. Everyone looked grim as if someone had died. Raj was called and the line was handed over to me. Raj said, "Yashi! I cannot continue this relationship with you. I would make some other arrangements for myself here. Please go ahead and withdraw your resignation."

My world came crashing again. For once, I demanded a reason but yet again was refused the same. Raj was the most disgusting man, a beast in the shape of a man. I hated him like I hated nobody else. I asked his parents and even Rohan, the reason for such a decision. They said, "He would only be able to tell you. You failed him as a wife."

I called up my brother. It was 11/April/2009 12:30 AM. I asked him to come and pick me. He was sleepy and confused. After all, I concealed all the torture I went through. He was taken aback. My brother started off right away and told me to hang in there. Strangely, I did not cry. I was dressed up in my night-suit and told the Khannas that I won't be able to live with them anymore. I took a decision for once in my life. Not to beg for this marriage to Raj. My next call was to Rachna, my Project Manager and a dear friend. I told her to put my resignation on hold. She understood my problem empathetically.

My brother called me as soon as he reached outside the house. the bitchy hip-looking lady instructed me to shed off all my jewelry. I was not allowed to wear even my Mataji's gold locket. The jewelry from my parents' side was all with her. I was in a bad emotional turmoil and jewelry or things were the last thing on my mind.

I sat in Bhaiya's car and the hip-looking lady said, "Monu, We would talk sometimes next week about this. We tried to stop her but she is not ready. She has a giant ego."

Bhaiya chose not to argue and drove me back to Ludhiana. Things did not cease to be turning ugly. Raj terminated his communication with me. I did not want to talk to him either. My parents still had a hope to save my marriage. Their hopes were shattered in the third meeting with Raj's family. I was fighting hard to find reasons to stay alive. I rejoined my job and tried to concentrate hard. I failed at times. My productivity decreased drastically but somehow, quality was still up to the mark.

My parents asked me "What next, Yashi!" I said, "Dad! I want a DIVORCE. That's it." They were still skeptical. I did not disclose the domestic violence I faced to them. They were already stressed out and I certainly did not wish to increase it.

In the meanwhile, I had posted an advertisement on the Infosys Internal bulletin board for sharing the accommodation. Swati joined me and I was extremely lucky that it was her and nobody else for she was a lady with an immense strength in her head and thoughts which could challenge even the Almighty. She was a witness to the downfall I faced in my married life.

I even developed certain habits which I never cherished earlier. I think my "SELF" got distorted. I was punishing myself now. I was doing things I had never done or thought I would do. I started drinking and even smoked for a while. I thought that being focused has got me nowhere, so let's see what happens if I lose it.

Then came the night when I absolutely gave up. I planned to drown myself in the Sukhna lake and even booked a cab to reach there. I composed a suicide note on the email and did not know whom to send it to. So it got saved in Drafts. I was in the cab. It was very late. I paid the cabbie, made my final few calls to all those who mattered. I was walking down the line separating the water from the road. I looked up one last time for a signal and what I saw was something I had forgotten

122

completely in my marital problems. It was MAHTAAB. I stopped. I felt him next to me and something vibrated in my pocket. It was Rahul's Mama. "Yashi Beta! I hope you are OK. I am sorry I called you at this hour. I just wanted to tell you that we have decided to open a nursing home in Rahul's memory in a village near Ludhiana. It would make him immortal. You are the one who matters the most to us, so breaking this good news to you in the first place.

MAHTAAB asked me to survive and live once again. He told me in his own special ways that he wants me to fight and not give up. I listened to him and returned. I promised him I would never even think of a suicide again. I shared the sequence of events with Swati. She made me look at things from a perspective that I thought never existed. She made me believe that I am lucky that this happened at such an early stage. It could have been worse with a baby around. I tried to come out of it. I was trying very hard, with psychological counseling, anti-depressants and never ending support from Family and friends.

Garima and Guncha, my friends and cubicle mates tried their level best to keep me afloat. Their silly jokes threw a smile at my dead face sometimes. Gradually, I smiled more often. Ridhima made my lunch routine proper. She belonged to Delhi and brought yummy Paneer bhurjee (cheese dish) every Monday cooked with immense love by her mother. I found pillars of strength all around me. I started seeing people who were even less fortunate that I was. My family got back to normal and we sued them. I was hoping the law to teach them a lesson for lifetime.

But I took my lesson, after this betrayal. It was somewhere in end of July, a friend suggested that I should do something that interests me. What could have been better than writing? I took the advice and wrote "Reflections." The critical and appreciation mails were much more effective than the anti-depressants I was on. I was out of my depression by August.

The law taught them a well-deserved lesson. When I had enough of sulking and cribbing in my life. I thought of dusting it all off and waking up for a new dawn. But who would create that sunlight for me, I had no clue. I realized it all the answers were inside me. I just had to open my eyes and the sunshine was right there, nice and warm.

I was amidst my thoughts when I got a call from a friend in Bangalore who asked me, "What is wrong with your husband? Why has he written all crap about you on Orkut (a social networking site)." My world crashed. That beast had humiliated me the best he could. I wept and cried and yelled. I realized nothing was helping me at all. I went to Chandigarh and spoke to Smriti Sharma, who was a city reporter with a leading national daily. She happened to be a dear friend I had. She told me how I could use my computer skills to win this war against him. So, the test engineer in me came out and I took screenshots of each of the abuses hurdled on me and my character and saved those in a .zip folder. The next step was to use my writing talent and I wrote a very convincing letter to the Senior Superintendent of Police, cyber-crime cell, Chandigarh. He was very helpful and took the case forward. Legal summons were sent to them in Jalandhar.

Thanks to Smriti, their true ugly face was brought in front of the entire world. Next day, their deeds were on front pages of almost all the leading local newspapers. How they duped me and my family! How that guy went underground after spoiling my life! How they tried to demean me in public! I forwarded the copies of all my complaints to National Commission for Women, Domestic Violence cell, National Human Rights Cell, The President's office, The Prime Minister's office. My voice was heard and I was contacted by Moska Najib, the overall producer of BBC-Asia. She promised to involve international media in my fight. My fight was no more my own. I felt I represented each and every Indian girl, who gets duped by NRIs and their families. I had a moral obligation to stand up for each one of the girls, who face dowry harassment and domestic violence. I was the voice of an Indian woman who once thought that ending her life is the best she can do for herself and the world.

I was wrong; **ending one's life is no solution**. I was thankful for all the support I had. I never would have known that Yashi was so strong if she would not have been through all this. I continued my job at Infosys and found amazing support from all directions. Law taught them a lesson. He was deported from UK and the court split us up. They were ordered to return my jewelry and other belongings. They played their cheap dirty tricks then as well. The hip-looking lady tried to replace genuine diamonds in my jewelry with fake ones. The con did not go unnoticed and the court rebuked them for their mischief.

I was happy that it was over. On 21st July, 2010, I got divorced and achieved victory over not only them but over myself too, in a way. On the same day, another friend of mine named Charu gave birth to a beautiful daughter Sanvi (means Goddess Laxmi). For some reason, I share a special bond with Sanvi. She epitomizes liberation to me.

Now, I am full of life and zeal. I don't overindulge in alcohol or anything anymore. I have started valuing my life like I never did. Due to my good performance at work, my HI Visa for USA was initiated and I am looking forward for a great career ahead of me.

I was in Chandigarh DC of Infosys before coming to USA. Everything is same but Mahtaab is gone or I must say, I don't see him physically though, he is here by my side, helping me in making the right choice of words for "Reflections" and helping me in replying appropriately to all my critics as well as admirers.

I know that I am one of the very lucky few, who had the touch of love in their life. I can spend the rest of my life without his physical presence but can never forget him and his eyes. I watch the reflection of the moon every night in the DC's swimming pool and smile at him. It has never happened that he forgets to return my smile.

Today, as I conclude this story, I know many questions would rise. But Yashi is prepared to answer all of them now. I did not write this to gain sympathy of any kind. When you have support of friends and family, you do not need sympathy. I am a stronger person than I ever could have been. I feel like Gold at heart, which has to melt itself before it can take up the design. "If God brings you to it, He brings you through it." Is what I believe. I conquered my alcohol problem with huge efforts on the part of Swati, Gagan, Ridhima, Garima, Guncha, Shruti and many other friends.

I wish to thank all of them through this little effort I have put in. I am able to face the world with much more courage than I could ever imagine. Life is not easy; this is what my life has taught me. At the same time, I know now that it is only as difficult as we make it for ourselves.

As far as love is concerned, I know there is someone who is waiting for me and who is right for me.